Running To Normal

Running To Normal

Sandra Clark

iUniverse, Inc.
New York Lincoln Shanghai

Running To Normal

iUniverse, Inc.

For information address:
iUniverse, Inc.
2021 Pine Lake Road, Suite 100
Lincoln, NE 68512
www.iuniverse.com

ISBN: 0-595-32558-0

Printed in the United States of America

This book is dedicated to all those kind souls, especially my family, who have stood by me in my search for myself.

Contents

Introduction

I remember the day I finally knew for sure; it was a sunny summer day in 1999. The final days of the 20th century (not really, but that was what everyone was saying) were coinciding with a suicidal depression brought on by decades of self delusion and the perpetration of a personal role that I felt I could no longer maintain.

I was literally sick unto death of the way I existed in the world, and had absolutely no idea how to relieve my pain. But for the love of my children I think I would have gladly ended my life. Instead I began a period of intense soul searching; a hunt for the absolute truths about myself and my past.

Over the years, I'd known there were some embarrassing aspects of my history and they were always there in the back of my mind, nagging for attention. Yet my shame led me to deny them and instead work as hard as I could present to the world the person I thought I should be, instead of the person I am. In fact, there in that terrible summer of 1999, I was finally able to contemplate the idea of who I really am for the first time. Those embarrassing aspects—*the root cause of my shame*—was that I wished I'd been born a girl.

I knew then that I'd chosen a dead-end path. In my youth when confusion had reined, instead of declaring to the world 'this is who I am', I instead chose to be the person everyone expected and wanted me to be. I ran headlong to 'normal'.

And on that sunny humid day I knew I was a transsexual, though I'd done a largely excellent job of convincing myself otherwise, not to mention never giving anyone in my adult life but my wife any hint of the turmoil in my soul. How did I get to this place where I was considering such a fundamental shift in my way of interacting with the world? Why did this happen to me? Why could I not *change* my mind and be the man I always thought I should be when I'd strived toward that goal with more vigor and purpose than nearly any other thing in my entire life? How does one go from being a late 20th century man to, if not *being* a woman, then at least living the life of one? Did I really want that, or was this just an aspect of some insanity? Did being a transsexual mean I *had* to go through a transition to living as a woman, or could I somehow integrate the truth and continue to appear to the world as a man?

There were a million questions in my mind and they all revolved around a frightening truth; a truth that had in fact been there the whole time, but hidden; shrouded in shame, guilt, and denial. Over the years since 1999 I solved most of those problems and on the way began to remember how I got there. I learned that Gender Identity Disorder (GID) has been a part of all cultures in recorded history and affects thousands worldwide. I learned that GID was and is treated differently in non-Western cultures and that the shame and disgust I felt with myself was a product of the society in which I was raised.

As free persons we get to make choices. A fundamental choice is whether to be honest with other people and declare who one is, or to instead craft an 'acceptable' persona in order to blend in with society. I made a largely unconscious choice to blend in with everybody else. Perhaps by reading my story others will be able to find the courage to be who they really are.

PART I

Normal: *Conforming to a type, standard, or regular pattern...*

◆

Merriam Webster's Collegiate Dictionary, tenth edition

1

Beginnings

Like any child I just was. My first memories are of playing with my sister and brother, being fed, taking a bath, and being with my mother. I have no early recollections of my father; he was nearly always at work.

Mom was very affectionate. She sang and read to us daily and gave us cookies too, my favorite food! I am the middle kid. My brother Scott was a newborn when my memories began in 1963. Playing with my sister was my primary activity. Though she is three years older we did everything together. We bothered the apartment maintenance guy, went door to door at all the neighbor's houses and played with other kids on the street.

Roberta was my one special friend. She and I played pretend games and she was always the boss. I don't remember the extent of these games but Roberta was in charge. I happily agreed to do whatever she required to make the game go the way she planned.

My sister, being older, went to school though I was still too young to attend. All of the kids on our street except me were girls and we played together daily after school. A well-worn family tale retells the story of one boring day when I asked my mother, "Mom, when am I going to turn into a girl so I can go to school too?"

I never believed I was a girl. I could see for myself just by looking in the mirror that I was a boy. Plus my parents told me so. I had no confidence or ability to contradict them. They were the gods of my life. I only knew that I did not feel like it *seemed* other boys felt.

As a wise friend kindly told me after I informed him in 2001 of my transsexual condition, "I'm glad you've understood this. The ways of the human mind are far more complex than we can ever truly know."

While I have no doubt that some transsexuals did and do have the clarity of mind at a young age to understand that their bodies should have been female (or male), I also know that the environment one experiences combined with the biological makeup of the individual will create unique responses to everything.

For me the feeling of strangeness was unnamed—un-explored. It just was, and it grew stronger and more profound over time. Since I've come to grips with all of this, I've remembered some things I had learned to forget. I now know that when I was 3-4 years old, I went into my mother's room and opened her drawers. There I found her nightgowns. Mom wore silky, diaphanous ones much like Mary Tyler Moore wore on the *Dick Van Dyke Show*. I would touch these and hold these to my face. They felt so good. Mom wore these at night when she tucked me in. I don't remember if I put them on, but I would go back to those drawers often to look and touch.

We moved often when I was little. My father was a struggling insurance agent and he kept looking for better and better jobs. Consequently, from my first memories in Redwood City California to junior high school, we lived in eight houses covering as many different schools. Shortly after my earliest memories we moved to Monterey California. There I began kindergarten in the neighboring town of Pacific Grove. I was very excited. I loved school from the first day and did until high school. I have very few memories from this time. But like most kids in the early sixties, I watched too much television. *Popeye* was my favorite cartoon.

I remember one day saying to my mom, "Can you make me some spinach so I can be as strong as Popeye?"

"Well honey, are you sure you want some spinach? I'm not sure you'll like it."

"I think it's important for a boy to be strong like Popeye, don't you Mom?"

Boiled spinach was truly the worst thing I had ever eaten, but I choked down a few bites and ran right out to see if I could uproot the huge palm tree in the courtyard of our apartment complex.

I felt I needed something special in order to be the boy the world expected. Of course I did not know this at the time. I just wanted to be admired and seen as a great boy. This was important to me and remained so until just the last few years. In order to combat that feeling of strangeness, of somehow being too different, I felt that if I simply gave people what they wanted and expected from me, I would be all right. At first I was not very good at it. I did not understand what they wanted and also did not have the mental fortitude to act contrary to my nature.

I could see how the other boys at school acted; competitive, aggressive, attracting attention to themselves, and dominating in conversation and social settings. I remember this beginning in first grade. Boys would stand out on the playground at recess and break pencils to impress the girls. They played 4 square and dodge ball with a fierce drive to win. I preferred to watch yet I also thought, 'I should be doing these things, too.' I knew immediately that I was nearly a complete failure at sports. Of course, many boys have little talent for sports. This does not mean their brains are female. It just means their talents lie elsewhere. I did not know I was a transsexual. I didn't even know the word. I only knew I did not feel like the other boys seemed to feel.

I longed to be an athlete but had no innate ability. Boys only want to play with boys who know how to play. So if you don't know how they won't pick you to play. Catch 22—if I could play, they would pick me, and if they would pick me, I thought I could learn to play. *I could not play, so I could not play.*

One thing I could do was break pencils like the other boys. I would stand on the playground and revel in the attention of the girls. A few would gather around and watch as I broke pencils for them.

We moved after first grade. It was a move short in miles but to a kid it might as well have been a thousand. Seaside was the next town over on the Monterey peninsula. It was the poorer cousin to Monterey which even then in the mid-sixties was beginning to become the trendy place it is now. We rented a house at the top of the hill in Seaside just two streets down from the major Army installation of Fort Ord.

Second grade contains my most vivid memories of having the crap beat out of me. For some reason I was seen as the school punching bag. One fellow in particular, Scott (a 4th or 5th grader), took a particular dislike to me and made it a point to find me every day after school. If I was smart (and I usually was) I could find him first and skirt his line of vision the long way round to home. But on some occasions he would find me and taunt, jab, and punch me all the way home.

One day he caught me at a small playground. In addition to various punches, head locks, and other indignities, he threw a swing at me so hard he knocked the back off of my new front tooth.

Later that year he was the instigator for my most vivid lesson in what I needed to do to please my father. That day he followed me home. Finally right in front of my own house, he jumped me and began to punch for all he was worth. We were rolling in the street and Scott was, of course, winning. My father pulled up in his black 1958 Buick, home from work early for once. I recall the feeling of relief that came over me as he got out of his car. 'Now I'm saved', I thought. But he just stood there and watched, waiting to see how I would handle myself.

In 1968 this was a common approach to raising a boy. It was seen as 'making a man of him'. I'm sure my father had little idea how uncomfortable I was acting the way boys were supposed to act. He was probably aware that I was somewhat of a sissy and not very aggressive. I simply had no idea why boys wanted to fight, to push, or to beat on each other, even when they were friends. That culture of violence and aggressiveness was completely foreign to me. If I'd had words for my then schoolmates they would have been Rodney King's: can't we all just get along?

After second grade we moved again. It was just a few miles away but a much better neighborhood. Third grade was to contain a major awakening for me. The boys here were much less aggressive (but it did not stop a neighborhood rock fight that put a few stitches in my head) so I was a lot more open in school. There I met one girl in particular, Melanie. I wanted nothing more than to spend all my free time with her. We often spent recesses and lunch together.

One day I asked her to come over after school so we could walk my dog. Melanie arrived and we walked the dog back over to the school, which was only a few blocks away. We had a good time. However my sister saw me with her and I knew I was in for it. My sister is a wonderful person, but every 11 year old will tease a younger sibling.

At dinner that night she happily sang out to our parents, "Stewart has a girlfriend!" I was not surprised that she did not keep my secret. My mother, though, began to tease me about this. "Stewart has a girlfriend? Stewart has a girlfriend?"

My mother's teasing became a wildfire memory for me. Even today, long after I've placed that event within the context of my life and relegated it to its proper place, I see that scene as if filmed through a fish-eye lens, my mother's face overly large and threatening, "Stewart has a girlfriend? STEWART HAS A GIRLFRIEND?"

Over the years I've thought a great deal about this event. I was taunted for liking a girl, something people tend to do at any age. However, I had an out of the ordinary reaction: I was completely devastated by the teasing. I felt totally betrayed by my mother. From a sister one expects teasing. We'd done it to each other for years. But when it came from my mother I was crushed.

It's impossible for me to put the exact right words on paper describing how odd I felt as a child, how out of place. Events would take place and I was as if in a storm without protection. Shortly after the incident with my mother we moved again; about 30 miles away to Salinas.

For the next 3-4 years I thought and dreamed of Melanie. She seemed to be the perfect girl and I had been ridiculed and humiliated for liking her. 'Why,' I continuously asked myself. 'Why was I not supposed to like girls? What is wrong with girls?'

Shortly after we moved to Salinas, I made a conscious decision to shut off all emotions. I just could not understand my mother's behavior. There were too many behavioral incongruities and I could no longer bear the pain. I've come to believe that my extreme reaction and subsequent focus on this one event was probably due to a longer standing pattern of not being able to understand. I did not know what confused me. If I'd known, I would not have been so confused! But I knew the confusion made me miserable. I was sad and could not seem to reconcile the conflicting messages. So I closed down. It must have been the one solution I could employ that would give me some control.

From that moment on I refrained from hugging, kissing, touching of any kind. Extreme joy or sadness was strictly avoided. And most definitely NO CRY-ING! Surprisingly, my school life began to get a little better. By being cold I projected something masculine, so I was only avoided. This was certainly preferable to being hunted. Yet I still longed to be included. The boys played sports and I could not and the girls stuck to their own kind. In my isolation I found music.

My sister had been offered piano lessons, and before long I wanted to take them as well. It was agreed I would begin studying with the local teacher, Mrs. Warziki. She was a patient, beautiful lady who kept a spotless house and was a fine teacher.

In the following school year, all 4th grade kids could join the band and I wanted to do that more than anything. They sent home a form where you could indicate your preference for musical instrument: violin, trumpet, drums, saxophone, etc.

"Dad, dad, the school will teach us to play instruments," I screamed as he arrived home from work one night. "I've got the form right here. Can I join the band dad? Huh? Can I?"

"Why sure, son. You can join the band. What instrument would you like to play?"

I had always been attracted to the patriotic picture of the three revolutionary warriors: the one with the flag, another with a drum and the last with a fife. "I want to play the flute!"

"*What?*" My father's voice roared. Do not all children grow up to recall their parent's voices as being on a par with God? "*No*. No son of mine is going to play a flute! You're going to play the trumpet!" We rented a trumpet.

Like most beginning band students I was terrible. Mr. Wigglesworth tried his best, but he had 24 or so of us with which to work. It did not help that the most popular kid in school was also learning the trumpet, and he learned it very fast. He was also the best athlete at school, a 4th grade whiz at the piano and, to top it all off, the son of my mother's boss at work. I glommed onto him as much as I could. He was as kind as he could be to a dork (me), but I really didn't fit into his social circle. I could not play sports and I could not play the trumpet or piano near as well as he did. In fact, I thought he was better than I was at everything. I began to put a lot of pressure on myself to play better, but remained the slowest learner and one of the worst players in elementary school.

At the end of 4th grade we moved again. Not far, only a few blocks, so I did not have to change schools. But moving is always somewhat traumatic, and it was there that I first began to see my sister treated differently than my brother and myself. One day dad came home from work early to find her in her bedroom with a boy from school. I must have blocked out the memory because my sister tells me she got a beating for that and I was there to see it. I only remember the tension: very thick and very bad.

That year of fifth grade there were only one or two truly memorable incidents for the whole year. The most vivid one was that my underwear began to bother me. For some reason the flap they put in jockey shorts was in a bad spot for my anatomy. My penis kept slipping through the access slot and getting stuck. It did not hurt so much as that it just annoyed me. I had never been aware of the organ much to that point, but now I could not stop pulling at my pants to readjust myself. My father would see this and get quite angry. Years later I learned he'd been severely beaten for masturbating when he was young. After his mother caught him for the umpteenth time, she took him to the doctor and insisted he be circumcised. I suppose he always agreed with the adage, 'anymore that two shakes and you're playing with it.' In fact, he liked that joke. I never really found it funny.

That year was also the first time I tried to play sports. The only organized sports one could play in the 1960s were Pop Warner football and Little League baseball. In that spring of 1970 I went out for Little League. I'd tossed a ball around with my dad over the years so I knew how to throw and catch. Plus, I had a bat with which I'd learned to hit a ball when I threw it up in front of myself. But I'd never really hit pitched balls let alone played defense.

Practices were from 5pm to 6:30 daily. When we got to our first practice game they sent me to the plate. There was at least one person on base. I looked in at the pitcher. I knew enough to watch the ball. He threw it and it looked good so I swung. Crack! The ball went flying to the outfield so I ran and ran, all the way around the bases.

"Geez, you just hit a home run!" People were slapping my back. This is great, I thought.

The next time up there were people on base again with a similar result though not a home run. After the game guys were coming up to me left and right. "Stewart, you got 6 ribbies; that's amazing! I had no idea you could play!"

It truly felt great to be included, but each day that week I noticed something that bothered me very much. By the time I got home after practice my father had already been there for dinner and left again for his evening appointments. Being an insurance agent, he worked from 8am to 11pm. Most days he stopped at home for dinner, which was around 6pm. I played another week of Little League then quit. Not even some success at sports and inclusion in the club of boys could make up for what I really needed; to see my dad, if only for a few moments a day.

The next summer we moved. Again, just a few blocks, but now I had to go to a new school. This turned out to be both good and bad. I made some real friends there. Two boys were nice, Sheldon and Klaus. Klaus's parents were German and quite old fashioned. One day he invited me to his house. I was always wary around adults so said nothing in hopes that his mother would not notice me. The next day he told me I could never come over again. His mother was outraged that I did not introduce myself or even say hello. She was right; I was very rude, although I was not really aware of that at the time.

Sheldon was a small, wiry boy. I always remember him when I see a Jack Russell terrier. He, like them, was intelligent and curious. In school we had a great teacher, Mr. Loucks. Teachers like Mr. Loucks cannot exist in this world any more. He lived in the same neighborhood with us and we were often invited to come over to his house and watch him work in his workshop, or go into his house with him alone, or use his bathroom if we needed. In today's world this type of mentoring is far too dangerous for a male teacher. All it would take is a panicky parent or a child needing to use the teacher as a scapegoat and a great career could be over in a moment.

Sixth grade was also a turning point for me. I learned what a penis could do besides bother you or empty your bladder. One of the neighborhood boys showed me and I have a vague memory of him doing more than demonstrating on himself. Perhaps it's just a dream. I do remember finding it pleasurable, yet shameful. How is it that kids just *know* that an activity that has never been discussed is something for which to be ashamed?

Another turning point was girls. Every sixth grade boy begins to notice the girls. I remember one girl having what I considered to be the largest breasts I'd ever seen. Girls also kept to themselves much more. By that time my emotional distance had become an entrenched pattern of behavior. I was quite good at not knowing what I thought about myself. I did not question why Jim (my mom's boss's son) did not care to play with me, I just accepted. I did not question why I had been beaten up so much when I was younger, I just accepted. I did not question why my father was so angry with my sister, I just accepted. It was at this time that I became acutely aware that girls were completely different from me. But who was I? What was I? Don't all kids ask these questions? They are not unique to a transsexual.

I did begin to learn more and more about giving others what they want; about giving them a set of behaviors and actions that allowed them to be comfortable with me. I realized I needed to be as much like others as possible. I think this is just standard behavior for many young children. One story in particular illustrates my attempts to fit in.

In 1971, red windbreakers were all the rage. Most of the kids had them. I did not. I pestered my mother until she gave in and took me out to get one. In a great hurry, as she had many other things to do, we dashed into the department store and grabbed the first red windbreaker we saw.

I was in heaven. Now I would be accepted. Now my classmates would see me as OK. They had not treated me badly, but neither had they been very nice. One of our two teachers (not Mr. Loucks) could never understand that my name was not Steven. All year long he called me Steve. This was very funny for the other kids. So the red windbreaker was important to me.

As I strutted around the school the first day I had it, I just knew I was now OK. In the lunch line that day, a group of 3-4 girls just ahead were giggling and looking furtively in my direction. Finally one of them could not contain herself any longer.

"That's a nice red wind breaker you have. Especially the darts!" Great gales of laughter broke over that group…and then the next group…and finally the whole line realized there was something funny about me. I suppose that most of the boys were like me and had no idea what a dart was, but it was obviously something to be laughed at and they could tell I was terribly embarrassed, which of course made it the perfect moment for everyone to laugh.

My poor mother was very stressed at this time. On top of a 6th grader who was mad because of darts, her 3rd grade son was the type to bring home every living thing he could find. One day he noticed some frogs in a sewer. These were suburban sewers with big iron grates that covered the holes. Down about 6 to 10 feet were the frogs. Scott wanted those frogs very badly and as he was looking at them, a large older kid came along and offered to lift that grate for him. Scott took out his hook on a string, which he always carried and proceeded to lean into the sewer to snatch them. As he pulled himself out of the hole, the big kid dropped the grate.

It was later weighed to see exactly how much had dropped on him. Over one hundred pounds of cast iron fell squarely on the fingers of his right hand. I happened to ride up on my bike just moments later. I remember seeing him pull his hand away from the sewer, not knowing exactly what I was seeing. When I got to him tears were running down his face, but he made no sound. It was the only time I've ever seen a completely silent cry. I asked what was wrong but he said nothing, only began walking home holding up his right hand.

My sister was there and was immediately panic stricken. She called the police. One of Salinas' finest showed up a half hour later. "Great," we thought, "everything will be all right now."

"Put some ice on it," he said, then got in his car and drove away. Now, one could not mistake this for an ordinary injury. When I rode up to Scott on his way home, even I noticed that his fingers were flat. A normal finger is fairly rounded. Scott's were thin like Popsicle sticks.

By the next day he was at Stanford Children's Hospital where he stayed for over three months. My mother was there with him during the week while the rest of us stayed home.

I discovered later that my mother felt terribly guilty about what happened to Scott because she believed that if she had been home, somehow it would not have happened. In fact, that was just the way kids played in 1971. We went out and did stuff and then came home. Parents did not chaperone kids everywhere. The message was, "go out and play. Have a good time!" So even if she'd been home, its likely Scott would have been out playing in exactly the same spot anyway.

Although I remember many things from this time, I recently discovered I'd repressed many memories too. Perhaps it happened when my mother was away so much in Palo Alto, but it was at this time that I began going into her closet to look and touch. I had not done this since Redwood City and I don't remember if in 1971 I was aware of those earlier Redwood City memories. Mom had pretty clothes and wigs as well. I would take some of the clothes down and try them on. I just looked; just played. I can remember feeling good. I liked this and looked forward to being able to do it again. However, I knew I was not supposed to do it and felt bad that I wanted to. I had become so good at hiding from myself, that I can now remember thinking, as I finished putting all of her clothes away, "I was in here for a genuine purpose. I had business; *boy* business." I was able to not think about those stolen moments when I was in my other life. I was learning the fine points of *disassociation*.

The dictionary lists this for disassociation, 'to detach from association'. To me, in the context of transsexuality, it means a person who is able to detach the part of their mind that dresses and feels feminine from the part that must live out each day in the world. That was what I began to learn to do in sixth grade. Actually I had been learning it for a long time, yet in 6th grade it became directly associated with cross-dressing and feeling feminine. I could go for a few days without thinking about those things and the feelings they brought up, then something would make me aware of that part of myself and from then until when I had dressed, I was consumed.

The women in my life were being treated poorly, my sister especially. About this time she began to run away. She was fed up with the rules and a perceived lack of love and would take off. One horrific scene that curiously both Scott and I repressed for many years happened at this time. I cannot remember if it was before or after Scott's accident, but I know he was there because he and I both stood and watched in horror.

My father was angry with our sister for something. I do not know what. He began to slap and punch her. She fell back into an armchair and while she attempted to block the blows with her arms, he lashed out with as much anger and purpose as any kid that ever beat on me. We were all terrified. If ever I needed a lesson in keeping my shameful secret, I got it that night. She snuck out of the house after we'd all gone to bed and even though my parents called the highway patrol to arrest and detain her, she escaped the Salinas valley. She ended up at my mother's brother's house in LA. For the next six months, she lived there and went to school (doing pretty well, too.)

Actions give out messages without words. The unstated message to Scott and me was, 'keep in line, or you're out of the family'. Some messages are more forceful and clear when delivered without words. I've spoken with my mother a few times about this night. She said, and I truly believe her, that there was no intent to deliver any message to Scott and myself. She too felt a victim of my father's anger and has chided herself for years for not acting to protect her daughter. But after that night, as much as I could, I kept in line. Which is to say, I never told them what I was doing or how I felt.

◆　　◆　　◆

Junior high began with more changes. Although we were still in the same house, I was required to take a bus for the first time. At that time, the Salinas Valley was a farming town. Big agribusiness was king. To do most of the worst work, immigrants were brought in from Mexico. They were paid very poorly and treated even worse. *Gringos* were not necessarily nice to farm workers in everyday encounters.

My parents did not instill any particular prejudices. They said, 'Gypped' when they felt they'd been charged too much, and dad told off color racial jokes. However, the message was if a person was good, he or she would be treated well. My dad later became a role model for other managers at his firm, Prudential. He hired any kind of man; Latino, Black, Asian, or White. His only requirement was that they be good salesmen.

I like to think I treated most everyone the same. However my neighbors, the Galvez family, were a bit different. Undoubtedly the victims of the times and attitudes of the Salinas Valley in the early 70's, that family's kids had an extreme dislike for all white people.

Each morning I had to walk the three blocks to the elementary school where the bus would pick us up for the trip across town to the Junior High. But after the first week or so, I decided to wait a block away, because the Galvez kids and their friends would be ready with rocks. If I got close enough they hit me with them. I would wait that block away and just as the last few people were getting on I'd sprint to the stop and get on last.

Then, of course, came the gauntlet. The gauntlet was the narrow isle one had to walk to find somewhere to sit. All the kids were sitting as close to the aisle as possible, so that the bus driver would have to come back and force someone to move over and allow me to sit.

Being in Junior High meant I was becoming a man in my father's eyes. He decided I needed some toughening up. One day we went out to some of the beautiful hilly areas with an old shotgun he had inherited. We had two or three shells with us. He stopped the car and while Mom and Scott waited in the car, he took me out to shoot the gun. A 30 ought 6 shotgun is quite heavy for a puny 12 year old and I held it as best I could. He told me to look ahead and pull the trigger. The loudest sound I'd ever heard coincided with getting knocked onto my butt by a rifle stock and wondering why my mouth tingled so much. The recoil had sent the stock into my face, knocking off a third of my front tooth. So both of my front teeth bear the scars of masculinity training!

Another important event was one particular night at the movies. My father was an insurance agent. By that year of 1971, he'd become incredibly good at it, too. In 1971 he was the 81st best agent in the Prudential Insurance Company, which we felt was amazing and truly extraordinary given that Prudential usually had over 10,000 agents on staff at any one time. He was restless though, so always succumbed to the siren song of management. By accepting promotion, his income was determined by how well his staff of 5-6 agents did. As a private producing agent, he'd set his own salary by how much he sold, but in management he had to figure out how to get a staff of agents to do the job well in order for he himself to be paid. One of the ways he motivated them was to host parties and other fun group activities.

"Hey son, how would you like to come with me tomorrow night?"

"Sure dad! Where are we going?"

"We're going to see some movies. Would you like that? You like movies, don't you son?"

"Jerry, I wish you wouldn't," my mother said. "He's only a boy."

"Mom, I love movies. Besides, I never get to go anywhere with just dad. *Please* can I go," I whined.

We arrived at his office. The place was dark with all the desks moved to one side of the room leaving the chairs on the other side all facing the wall. An 8mm projector, half the size of the kind one found in public schools in the 60's and 70's, was set up on a desk. He said, "We're here, roll 'em."

"How odd," I thought, "movies at the office. And his entire staff here to watch them with us."

The film reels with tiny. There was no sound. "Weird," I thought, "silent movies in 1972." Then the movies began…and I was completely aghast: *Horrified*. I had no idea that that was what people did with each other. I do not remember having words in my head, but my father wanted to know if I was enjoying the movies. "Yes," I'd answer, afraid to anger him. At that age I never ever disagreed with him.

I saw hairy men with huge…*penises*…lying on top of flabby women who looked like they liked it. Many of the agents kept smiling and looking over at me. I did not know what they expected to see. They were missing the movies every time they looked over at me.

Afterward they all wanted to know what I thought of the films. "They were…*good,*" I said. Everyone laughed at that. There has always been something about the company of men that's shocked and disgusted me. A few years later when my father taught me golf we'd play with his business cronies and it would be the same kind of thing; all back-slapping and insulting each other.

I believe that though the memory of that night faded from my mind for decades, that evening of movies had a profound impact on my life. That was the defining moment when I learned what my revered father expected of me. The message was, 'you're a man and this is what men do. This is what you'll do.' Like it or not, that was my destiny. And in truth, I did not think about it much after that. Like most things in my life, I just accepted the reality as I found it. It's time to move again? "Okay." Scott and mom have to live in Palo Alto for 3 months. "Okay." We don't know where your sister is and we're not supposed to care too much. "Okay."

By the time of movie night I was on the cusp of puberty. I'd learned many things in my time on earth, but the majority of them remained secrets. I can say for certain that I wished for friends and acceptance. I wanted to be like everyone else; to be the same as my classmates, indistinguishable from the others. I'd had my fill of being different. The old saying goes 'be careful what you wish for, you just might get it'. I was not popular; not generally accepted. But that seemed to start at home. The fractured-ness of life emanated from there.

But then we got a chance; an opportunity to begin again and go to a place where no one knew us and have a fresh start. Shortly after movie night, dad accepted a much bigger promotion and we moved to San Jose, the ninth house and the eighth school since my memories began in Redwood City, and the last move we ever made as a family.

2

A Fresh Start

My parents bought a 2000 square foot suburban tract home in a former orchard for $32,000. We all loved it. Even my sister came back to us and we all moved together to our fresh start. As for mom, since State Farm would not transfer a woman who worked clerical, she had to go back to the very bottom of the pay scale in order to find work with them. She accepted a position for the least amount they were willing to pay anyone. This was another message I heard loud and clear about the second-class status of women.

San Jose was a nice town. It had better weather than the Monterey Peninsula, or at least we all thought so. We had the best and nicest house we ever had. Dad was ecstatic with his new job and mom was happy that he was happy. School, however, was a different story. I began at Caroline Davis Jr. High in the middle of 7th grade and immediately earned the nickname 'brain'. I suppose it was because I actually did the assignments and turned in the homework. I even knew many of the answers when the teacher would ask for a response. I raised my hand many times every day and through these grievous offenses, I earned the wrath of most of the boys in the school.

I did enjoy band very much. Miss Van Allen, a pretty woman in her twenties (maybe a bit older?) was kind and immediately recognized that I was one terrible trumpet player. She asked me to switch to the baritone, which I did and within ten minutes was more successful than I'd ever been with a trumpet. It's quite simple if you've played the trumpet; it's just a bigger mouthpiece. All of a sudden I could play like I'd never been able to. I stuck with that for months. In 8th grade she would hand me the French horn for the first time and although I was terrible at it, I did love it even more than the baritone.

◆   ◆   ◆

Like many suburban streets, ours had other young children in residence besides my brother and me. Down on the corner was a kid about Scott's age. Joe was a cocky kid, overly sure of himself in all things, especially athletics. He took an immediate dislike to my brother which left me rankled. Though I was fairly emotionally distant, I would have stood up for my brother if necessary. Joe thought Scott was kind of a sissy and thought I was kind of cool. Ah, irony! If only he knew. I think it was the three-year age difference. He showed me a deference I'd never received from anyone, and I quite enjoyed that.

While Joe would not play with Scott, I would play with Joe. We played catch with a baseball and mitts. We also shot hoops in his driveway.

"Come on Stewart, let's play 'horse,'" he asked the first time we played basketball.

"What's 'horse,'" I said.

"You've got to be kidding me! A sophisticated guy like you and you don't know what 'horse' is? Where did you grow up again?"

"Salinas, mostly," I answered. I was always amazed at Joe's command of male bravado, ego, and bluff. He talked like a teenager, and he was only nine.

"Dude, take this ball and throw it. If you make it I have to make the same shot. If I miss (but I won't), I get an 'h', and vice versa. We keep that up till one of us has spelled out the whole word—*horse, get it?*"

"Yeah, I guess," I said. I went first.

"Man! You suck," Joe said. "That wasn't even close. I am gonna' *smoke* your ass!"

Joe always won. I played because receiving attention was too fine a thing to predicate it on winning. We also played Frisbee, a game at which I seemed to excel for some reason. It seemed I was quite good at throwing things; the Frisbee, the baseball, and even the basketball, though my aim with the basketball was pretty bad.

After a few months I got Joe to let my brother Scott hang out with us, and they soon became friends. Increasingly they did stuff on their own without me. I felt left out but it seemed right somehow.

◆   ◆   ◆

I was used to school ostracism, having bus-riding hassles, and being ignored by the girls. When I wasn't playing with Joe, I spent many hours in front of the TV after school each day. Some days I would find myself there alone, and I'd know that Scott was out with Joe and my sister was gone somewhere for a long time; and I could not stay out of my mother's closet. She had beautiful things in which I still fit. It was at this point that I began to dress fully. I did not use make-up because I really did not know the first thing about it and I did not have a particular interest in it anyway, not to mention the worry about leaving a mess or somehow alerting mom to what I was doing. It was the thrill of seeing me dressed as a girl that was so wonderful. When I was brave enough to get out one of her wigs, then I felt the transformation the best. I would have a fashion show.

Too soon the time would come to go back to boy land. I never wanted it to stop, but I soon leaned what would make me take it all off quickly; what would leave me purged of the need to do it again, at least for a few days: masturbation. After the completion of that, I would feel like the biggest freak and pervert. I felt guilty and shameful and after I got everything back in exactly the right place, I would leave the room positive that I would never do that again. I did not want to do it again. In my mind it was wrong. The movies proved that I would be having sex with women, so I couldn't possibly *be* a woman.

There was a large window in my parent's room. It looked out over the tiny backyard toward other tract homes in the neighborhood. Little did I know that it looked right into the house of one of my classmates. I cannot recall her name, nor would I ever want to, for I'll always remember her and her friend as two of the cruelest people I've ever known. I do not think she ever saw me dressing for she would undoubtedly have broadcast that fact to everyone she could find, but I often wondered. Very soon after the move to San Jose, she tagged me with the moniker I lived with until high school—*Stewfag*. Lots of kids get called fag, queer, and sissy, but with me I thought they had somehow found me out. "How did they know that I liked to dress like a girl," I often thought.

As a 12-13 year old, I was not versed in the intricate differences between cross dressers, transsexuals and homosexuals. I had no inkling that my need, that the part of me that led me to my mother's closet, was the very core of my being and that much of my chafing at the role of boys in society was connected to that. I only knew that dressing as a girl relived *some* pain; *a* pain; and soothed my soul like a balm on my heart. But whenever I heard 'Stewfag' from them or their legions of friends, the guilt I felt at dressing and masturbating would re-surface, and my system would be flush with that shame to the point where it became my constant companion.

As I continued with my mind game of dressing, masturbating and believing I would never do it again, I began to have fantasies. I imagined myself being on the receiving end of a man's attentions. I do not remember being aware of a connection between the movies I'd seen and my interest. I only knew that my mind was going there with no help from me and I very much wished it would not. "See, I *am* a fag", I would think when these thoughts plagued me. I needed to know what that was like. What did a woman feel like when a man entered her? How could I ever experience that feeling too?

◆   ◆   ◆

One of the best aspects of living in San Jose was that nobody 'called me out' or jumped me. I had a yearlong period of enjoying relative peace in my life from moving to San Jose until the middle of my 8th grade year. Then a couple of brawny brothers moved into the neighborhood.

Mike and Ike were bullies. They insisted that younger kids cross the street to avoid them and play games they chose whenever demanded. They acted like dictators. Scott and Joe were particularly upset one day. Mike and Ike were doing their usual thing, when something in me just snapped. Perhaps it was the duality of my private and public personas, or maybe I had just developed a greater sense of justice and had decided enough was enough from these guys. When Mike got in my brother's face right in our own driveway, I hauled off and slugged him—*hard*. Immediately, my head was snapped back by his strong punch to my nose. But I was angry. I'd lost every fight I'd ever been in and at that moment I knew why. It was because I'd never been mad. This time was different. I hated what they did to people! I growled—I *screamed*—and charged him, tackling him around the torso and throwing him to the ground. My fist kept snapping into his face—2, 3, 4 times in a row. Then his leg wrapped over and around my waist and he pulled me over onto my back. I knew his fist was coming and it did, pounding my nose a few times. I retreated by scooching my head back into the crook of his legs and flailing my arms up at his stomach.

I caught a glimpse of my mother, brother, and sister standing on the sidewalk with horrified faces watching me actually mix it up with this piece of shit. Mike and I exchanged advantage a few more times. Then our neighbor arrived home in his car and he broke up the fight. We were like two dogs clingingly reluctant to stop killing each other. I truly wanted to kill him. I'd never been that angry in my life and though I was not winning, I don't think Mike was either.

My body hurt. My nose had that tingle and slight burning odor that comes from impact. I'd not shed a single tear. Once I got inside the front door though, I lost my composure completely and began wailing and flinging myself. I can vividly remember both hating that I'd fought him, and wishing I'd finished that *fuck* off once and for all. My mother tried to calm me down, but I had some boiling to do first. Once it was over, tears, wails, and hand wringing were all I could do. There was a silver lining to that fight however, Mike and Ike stayed on their end of the street and aside from two relatively minor incidents, it was the last fight I've ever had.

During that summer before high school, the first of those 'minor incidents' played out. I started noticing a guy hanging around our neighborhood. After a couple of days, I asked his name and story.

His presence was large, both in size and speech. "I'm Kent, from Chicago. I'm staying with my uncle for the summer. Who the fuck are you and why you askin' me questions?"

I got the message. "Um, I'm Stewart—I live here," I said, pointing to the house behind me.

"You're some kind a fag, Stewart," he sang. "Who's your boyfriend?" I turned around and went inside, saying nothing. I'd learned that, unlike dogs, the most vocal boys are often the most dangerous, and I wanted nothing to do with Kent.

Over the course of the summer I'd see Kent nearly every day and he'd have a choice word or two for me. Mike and Ike hung out with him and though they joined in for the easy laugh at my expense, they pretty much left me alone. Until one day, when I was cleaning the garage.

I looked up and Kent was standing over me sweating in the summer heat.

"Hey," he said.

I heard a genuine friendliness in his voice. I looked at him, taking stock of his manner and change of heart.

"Hey," I said.

"What are you doing?"

"Oh, my Mom told me I have to clean the garage today and…I kind of like it. There's all this junk I've not seen since we moved here from Salinas."

"Where's Salinas?"

"About an hour south of here. It's an ok town, but I like San Jose a lot better." I stopped, wondering how to go on and keep the conversation going; how to win him over. "Would you like to see this model I just finished? It really flies!"

"Um…Ok," he said.

We went in the house. I showed him a balsa wood airplane I'd spent dozens of hours building. "Do you want to go out and fly it with me," I asked him.

He looked at his watch. "I, uh, actually have to get going. My uncle is expecting me."

"Oh, alright."

We headed back downstairs to the garage. I stood at the door between the house and garage. Kent looked back up at me.

"Thanks. See you," he said and turned. Then he stopped. "Oh, I forgot something," and he spun back around and punched me right in the mouth. I'd gotten braces a few weeks before and I immediately felt a flood of blood filling my mouth. "God, what a fag you are," he shouted, loping off and laughing strongly. My father was in the house reading and came right over to the door.

"Oh Stewart, come here, let me help you." I was crying and he didn't even mind. I think he'd gotten the gist of the situation. My breath started coming in shorter and shorter gasps. I was getting very, very angry. Still raining blood, I jerked away from my father and stomped out to the garage.

"Son, where are you going with that baseball bat?"

"I'm gonna *kill* that shit!" I headed out to the sidewalk.

"What he did was very wrong, but I'm not going to let you ruin your life over this. Come back here. **COME BACK HERE.**" My father's raised voice always had a magical power over me. "Let me tell you what we're going to do," he said in a soothing voice.

He decided we'd go down and talk to his uncle. I knew exactly where Kent was living because I was the neighborhood paperboy, and everyone took the paper. We cleaned up and walked around the corner.

"Hello Mr. Jones, my name is Jerry Clark. Your nephew Kent was just at our house and hit my boy here. I'd like to talk to you about that."

"You've got exactly five seconds to get the ***fuck*** outta my face before I leave you worse than your sissy-shit kid there."

We left.

◆   ◆   ◆

I had always been, essentially, a loner. My favorite home activity (besides television and dressing as a girl) was model building. I had built every plastic World War 2 airplane model on the market and soon had graduated to the balsa wood types that actually flew. I built a huge glider with a six-foot wingspan. It looked so good I was afraid to fly it. But eventually, I launched it off the roof of the house and watched it soar down the street. Unfortunately, those things nearly always break with each landing, so I was constantly repairing it. I built many basic airplanes powered with rubber bands. Each took dozens of hours to complete with many detailed steps of construction. All were of the same style of construction as a real airplane.

My fascination with flight led me to beg my father for flying lessons. My paper route netted over $100 a month. I wanted to use the money to learn to fly gliders which kids could get licensed in at age 14. Dad agreed and twice a month he drove me the 45 miles on crowded bay area freeways to a glider port in Fremont. Sky Sailing airport no longer exists; a victim of the massive real estate boom of the 80's. But in 1973 and 1974, it was a great place. I would soar with an instructor in the Schweitzer 233; a two-seat trainer. I learned all the basics, but slower than either I or my teacher had expected.

Finally, after months of instruction, solo flight day came. This would take place in two stages: a quick flight around the airport and then a longer flight to more fully test my skills. The first flight around the airport went fine. Then I was towed off for the longer flight. I pulled the towline-release knob and set the Schweitzer 233 free at about 4500 feet. In my training we had often headed over to the nearby hills to catch lift off the ridge. If there were special weather conditions that caused this I had no idea what they were and never before worried about whether there was lift or not.

I nosed the plane over to the 3500-foot peak on the east side of the bay. The peak was rocky topped green spot. I had seen the instructor head straight for it and eventually the plane would rise. We would then turn and follow the ridge of the peak for a while, rising as we went. I continued to head toward the peak. In a glider, forward motion is created at the expense of altitude. One is continually falling to earth but in a controlled and efficient way.

The peak kept getting closer and closer and I knew the lift should hit any moment. I was ready with the controls to give the left rudder and pull back and to the left with the stick so the plane could follow the ridge. Closer still and no lift; and now I began to wonder, *"where is the lift?"* I could see details of the mountaintop. The design of the boulders and the green tufts of grassy patches were plainly visible. I was now truly worried.

"There's no lift! Hey, I'm going to hit this mountain unless I do something!" I immediately pushed the stick down and to the left. This dropped the nose and the left wing. At the same time I jammed the left rudder to the floor so the tail would follow the nose around. I was extremely close to the peak now and could see small rocks and individual blades of grass. I was looking over my shoulder at the peak as the nose came around. I knew I'd gotten the front of the plane out of danger but was worried about the tail. I could see that it was within a few feet of scraping the rocks. I pushed farther on the stick even though there was nowhere for it to go, hoping for more speed and fall to prevent stalling.

It was probably only 5-6 seconds after I decided there was no lift that I was racing in a dive down the mountain, though it seemed far longer. Once safe, I pulled the plane out and looked at the altimeter. I had lost well over 1500 feet in my foolish brush with death. I knew from experience that I probably did not have enough altitude to get back to the airport.

My teacher and I had discussed how in a glider, you could land in a pasture if you had to. But I had never done it, nor seen it done, nor heard of any pilot at the airport who had. Twenty tense minutes later I set up for the landing. I short-cutted the usual landing procedure in order to save altitude. Instead I went right to the approach and left off the air brakes. Air brakes are for properly preparing the plane for landing, but they do that by gently slowing the craft allowing for a gentle landing. I was coming in too fast. I thought I was going to make it. I'd made it far closer than I'd imagined I could. Finally though, I knew I would not make it and faced my fate of having to land while avoiding fences and cows. I managed to get the plane down only 100 yards from the end of the runway. I was completely mortified at my failure and embarrassed about my foolish attempt at finding lift. I was certain I'd be the laughing stock of the whole airport.

I ran the distance back to the field. My instructor just shrugged and said, "these things happen." He hopped into the tow plane, flew around the airport, and within 10 minutes the glider was back at its parking spot.

Yet I felt so bad about what I'd done that I never went back. I could not admit to myself that I was afraid to go back, but I probably was. For years I'd had a dream of being a Navy pilot and participating in aerial dogfights. The glut of war movies on TV and my acknowledged need to be more masculine drove me to see flying as a proof of manhood. Within a year of the glider solo flight I had stopped building models, and dropped the goal of going to Annapolis all together. I had found a new way to feel good about myself and it was better than anything that had ever happened to me before: I discovered a straighter path (so to speak) to my goal of being normal. *I finally learned how to get people to like me.*

3

Party Jock

I'd dreamed of having some semblance of popularity since my earliest days of school. From house to house; from school to school; I failed to find that peer acceptance. But finally in high school I figured out how to do it: become an athlete.

When one is young there are only a few sports one can play, at least in the 60s: baseball and perhaps football. I'd had my chance at baseball and never really could stomach football. But once in high school all sorts of more exotic sports were available, like soccer, track, basketball, and water polo.

My first attempt at a sport tryout was for the soccer team in my freshman year. Soccer I reasoned, being a relatively unpopular sport, would not have great players vying for spots on the team. Hence, I could get on the team and be seen as an athlete. I quickly realized the coach had his favorites already picked out. These guys could really play the game. For the rest of us, the rules were simple: run a mile in six minutes and you could be on the team. I actually surprised myself running the distance in around 7 minutes. Not bad I now know for an out of shape person. I did not play soccer.

In the summer between freshman and sophomore years, I heard of water polo. I did not know what it was, but it was even more obscure and unpopular than soccer. I went to an informational meeting and immediately went out for water polo. I was a fair amateur swimmer having loved pools all my life and was quickly one of the better 'scrubs' in the pool. Most of us freshman and sophomore kids were just learning the game. We learned to tread water the *right* way (the 'egg beater'), how to throw and catch the ball with one hand, how to *drive* with the ball (swim with your head up and have the ball move with you on the wave of water in front of your face) and elementary game strategy. In all the basics, I was ok except for game strategy. I simply could not understand the intricacies of passing to the hole and back out and keeping the ball away from the opponent to get it to your own people.

I was, however, enthusiastic. It now reminds me of music in that I started on trumpet and while eager was awful. It was the same story with water polo. In music I found my niche with the French horn, and in water polo I found my place in the goal. The object of the game is to score by throwing the ball into a cage with a net. This is defended by the goalie. It's really soccer in the water and I became the goalie. This I could understand; keep the ball from going into the goal and throw the ball back to our own players. That was my job. And I loved it. My talent for throwing things served me well here as I was often able to steal the ball from the opposition, or block a shot, then accurately pass the ball back to my teammates as they swam back the other way.

Finally, I was seen as a real person; an athlete. I had friends, or at least acquaintances, who believed I was just like them, and through their eyes I believed it myself. I became strong, especially in my legs, as the goalie must be able to agitate out of the water to the waist and stay there for a few moments in order to block the goal. This was my best trait, my strength. I did not do so well with actually blocking the ball, but I could get out of the water very well and pose a large obstacle to the other team scoring.

One particular day highlights the dangers of that job. As we warmed up for a game, my teammates were practicing shooting by doing so at the cage in which I worked, so naturally I practiced my job by trying to block their shots. Three guys in a row drilled me right in the nose. A water polo ball is about the size of a volleyball but much harder. It is made of tough leather that has a nap that increases one's ability to grip the ball when it's wet. I was in great pain for a few days, but athletes are told to shrug off pain and keep to the task. I did that and found out ten years later that I had at some time broken my nose. My guess is it was probably that day. I had my septum repaired in 1987 but was left with enlarged bony structure just before the cartilage begins.

I reveled in the attention and respect accorded to athletes, yet I was also very eager to have as many friends as possible. So I became involved with some people from the band. These people became my best friends. Athletics I did for status; the band I did because I loved it. The people I met there I truly liked and enjoyed.

One extremely positive aspect of my hanging out with the band kids was my involvement with the drum and bugle corps activity. Most people are familiar with marching band. Drum corps (as it's usually called) is much like that, except there are only brass and percussion instruments and a *color guard*. Color guard is an old military term that essentially means visual support of the program through the use of flags and other implements of color.

From 1975 through 1981, I was involved in that great activity. Kids 14-21 receive instruction on their instruments and the movements on the field. The field movements are far more difficult than those done in a high school marching band.

The local group, The Knight Raiders, took me on in mid-summer 1975, after the summer water polo season had ended. The horn line had 24 members. I played 2nd baritone (I played both low brass and French horn all through high school). We rehearsed each day from about 9am till dark at a nearby high school. I was really only there because my friends from band were in it and they'd called begging me to join. It turned out that the movements on the field are far more difficult if there are missing people and they'd never found that 24th horn player. I liked being able to 'rescue' my friends by filling that needed role. That sense of being the hero was important to me.

In a very short period of time, I had to learn not only the music (which had to be performed from memory) but also the field movements. The 'drill' as it's called, consisted of marching (a controlled kind of walking) in certain directions while keeping prescribed angles and distances from other people constant. Those angles and distances changed over the course of the show. There was no written map for them in those days. One learned them by rote, taught by the instructors and the other people in the drill who already knew what to do.

Soon, we boarded two leased busses and headed north to Washington and Oregon for 'tour'. Never before in my life had I had such a liberating and fun experience as that first tour with the Knight Raiders. It was like Disneyland all the time! Soon I absolutely loved rehearsals. The act of improving on our product was, to me, very exciting. Performances were even better. Only someone who has stood before thousands of cheering fans can understand the thrill of drum corps performance! We were a pretty poorly scoring group. Our results reflected the fact that our members were mostly high school kids, and most of them freshmen and sophomores. But we were enthusiastic.

When we were not rehearsing or performing, we were riding the bus to get from one show to the next. Those were even more exciting than the work because on the bus, girls and boys were thrown together in a largely unsupervised way. There was 'making out' as we called it; and even more. I experienced my first kiss on that 1975 Knight Raiders tour bus. A girl from the color guard had taken a liking to me.

There is something so completely satisfying about letting your body do what it is screaming at you to do. Though I now understand how I'm different and that I have been this way for most or all of my life, I had at that time a male body.

That's really the essence of the 'dysphoria' part of this condition; the discrepancy between the female brain and the male body. The male body is designed to do certain things and it's very, very difficult to control it. Like every other guy on tour, I woke up every morning with 'stiffness' and though in my case it was something I was ashamed of, I did not tell that to anyone else!

But there in drum corps I was experiencing a level of acceptance from others I'd never known. Buoyed by that, my gender issues faded to the farther reaches of my mind. When I thought of them at all, it was to think that cross-dressing was 'something I used to do'.

Our food was usually peanut butter and jelly sandwiches for lunch and canned spaghetti for dinner. We slept either on the busses or on the gym floors of high schools in the towns we visited. We showered in their empty summer locker rooms (usually with cold water as most water heaters were off for the summer). It was a kind of gypsy existence totally removed from reality, yet it was also more reality than many kids experienced during their summers off from school. Here we were, 65 or so kids whom, instead of spending the summer watching TV or goofing off, were perfecting (to the best of our abilities) a musical and physical regimen and performing it for hundreds and thousands of people across the west. How cool is that!

Well, we all thought it was extremely cool, and after the summer tour was over, we could not wait for the corps to begin their work toward the 1976 season. That summer of '76, we'd been told, the Knight Raiders were going back east to the 'big show'; the DCI world championships in Philadelphia PA!

We made that tour in 1976. I'd been promoted to lead baritone (being that I was so much better on baritone than on French horn) and we all had a great time. We came in next to last in the standings, but got to travel through about half the states in the union over the course of the summer. My most vivid memory of that tour was a day we spent not far from where I live now, in Toledo Ohio. We were booked into the big show in Marion Ohio, and were assigned a school at which to stay in Morral Ohio. The building was, by far, the oldest school I'd ever seen. It was one solid block of brick. There were eight classrooms; no gym, no cafeteria, and only one set of bathrooms. At some point, they'd added showers in the basement with girls and boys separated by a thin curtain, two showers in each area. The water had a strong odor of iron and dripped continually. The darkly stained drain housed dozens of cockroaches that would scurry away whenever anyone took a shower.

◆   ◆   ◆

Like many kids in the 70's, we experimented with drugs. Each school year weekend involved attempting to get drunk, high, or both if possible. Marijuana made me paranoid. When high, I thought everybody could read my mind and knew all my shameful secrets. It took a number of episodes before I could tell how much to smoke and not have such a bad reaction that I made a complete fool out of myself. While in my heart I thought I was guilty and shameful, my friends had no patience for that kind of behavior. We were all supposed to be sarcastic and apathetic; and of course, extremely sure of ourselves. Since a vast majority of my personality was created out of what I thought others wanted and expected to see in me, I was sarcastic, apathetic and acted sure of myself; except when I'd imbibed too much pot or beer.

Our parties became a magnet for rebellious teens from around the valley. There were few names spoken. Even if there were, most everyone was too drunk or high to remember. We'd listen to Pink Floyd's *Dark Side Of The Moon* over and over. After tiring of that, we'd move on to anything by Maynard Ferguson. That was true band geek chic; a stoner party with music by a legend of the big band era! We also thought Chuck Mangione was the 'be all end all' of instrumental performer/composers. Hey, it was the 70's!

We never danced. Dancing was too preppy, too mainstream. We were different; *cool,* like jazzers of the 50's but without goatees. We sat and *listened.* Conversation consisted of bragging or dreaming of having something to brag about. And, of course, we were all terribly eager to get laid.

The sex act was a constant topic of conversation in my circle. One night, a young girl, about my age as far as I could tell in my altered state, made her willingness to get close obvious. Soon, we ended up in a bedroom upstairs. I fumbled (who doesn't their first time).

She said, "Don't—*you know*—in me."

We rutted. Men's senses tend to close off while in that process. They temporarily 'lose their minds'. Robin Williams jokes that men are made with a brain and a penis, but only enough blood to operate one at a time, so perhaps I can't be blamed for not hearing the gathering outside the bedroom door. Like a scene out of *Porky's* or *American Pie* we exited the bedroom to applause, slaps on the back, and cheers. And I, stupidly (due to my 'good boy' upbringing) brought along the soiled sheets so I could put them into the laundry. This brought howls of laughter from all of my friends.

That was the first time I saw the dark side of giving people what they expected. Sometimes you get burned. Sure, I 'got off', as the saying goes. I was the first in my crowd to 'score' and was just about its youngest member at 15. But they teased me mercilessly for weeks over that. The girl's name was not common but had been used prominently in a well-known song. My friends would sing that song every time they saw me.

I can recall that the constant teasing reminded me of third grade all over again with my mother teasing me about liking a girl. Of course, the teasing was one part disgust and two parts envy (or maybe the other way around?). I learned that later, as an adult. But then, in the midst of the torment, all I could see and feel was the pain.

I withdrew from them a bit after that. I'd opened myself up too much. I also felt terrible about how I'd treated this poor girl. I knew she'd agreed. There was no doubt that our act was consensual. But I did not have a sense of pride over it. I was ashamed of myself.

I think the 3rd grade teasing by my mother and the teasing after losing my virginity brought out feelings of shame because of what I am; because of my gender dysphoria. I had no names for those feelings then, and I had learned well to dissociate my cross dressing episodes from all the rest of my life, so I was at no risk of drawing any connections between the two. In other words, I stood no chance of learning something vital and important about myself!

But while still in high school, I realized I was growing out of the need to do everything my friends did. By my senior year, I attended parties much less and got high far less often. I realized I did not like myself at all when doing that. I was also very much under the influence of my parent's philosophy of 'positive thinking'.

Mom and Dad were both in the insurance business. It is famous for promoting any psychological program that purports to get more business out of its employees. My parents worked at and believed in these programs. I began to do so as well. At first, it was due to having little choice. My folks, in their zeal, went so far as to not allow negative emotions to be expressed. If one of us came home with a problem or just 'bummed out' on the day, we were quickly heard then told to drop it, get over it, and not to bring such negativity into the house. Repression was the order of the day. The 'act as if' principal ruled. 'Act as if' states: if you feel bad, *act as if* you feel great and soon you really will.

I feel strongly that many of the things they taught and espoused are good for humans. We do largely become what we think about most and we cannot dwell on the reverse of an idea. For example, it does little good to tell somebody to not do something. It will get better results to ask people for exactly what you want. I can prove it to you. Ready? ***Don't think about a watermelon***. The mind does not comprehend the 'don't' part, only the image. We live in images.

However, by making certain thoughts off limits, I learned to repress those thoughts. I learned to deny feelings. The lesson was 'if they're negative, you need only act as if they're not there, and they soon won't be'.

By the time I'd faced a suicidal depression at age 39, I finally realized that one cannot deny and repress emotions: to be dealt with they must be felt. But as a young 17 year old, I was able to play the game of positive emotions only pretty well.

Since we were not raised with religion, I was an agnostic/atheist (depended on what day you asked me). Yet young people crave structure, order, and systems. Without religion (which some might say is a form of cult), I became vulnerable to a cult. The cult I found was the objectivists, a.k.a.: Ayn Rand's philosophy.

My mother was a huge fan of Rand's novels. I'd read *The Fountainhead* and *Atlas Shrugged* and not only enjoyed the writing, but also completely bought into the philosophy. I purchased all of her non-fiction and read that, believing myself some kind of superior being. She's very much like Nietzsche that way.

This philosophy was attractive because it elevated the individual to superior status. Her characters succeeded in spite of others, yet they were good, if lonely, people. I was lonely; yet felt that if I followed her tenets, I too would be good. If you've read her you may know what I mean.

◆   ◆   ◆

In my senior year I served as captain of the water polo team. They also elected to award me the most inspirational player plaque. At the time I thought of it as the 'worst player you feel sorry sucks so bad' award. While I loved water polo, I detested the swim team. I had only participated for two years in order to remain eligible for the water polo team. Once water polo was no longer the carrot I felt no need to continue being beaten by the swimming stick. Instead, I tried out for the spring musical. The school decided on *L'il Abner* for the spring of 1977. That forgettable musical drawn from the comic strip (which none of us had ever read) was to be our ticket to high school stardom!

Quite a few of my band geek friends tried out with me. None of us had sung in choir or done any singing before. But the musical looked like fun. Amazingly, we were all cast in some prominent parts. I was cast as the lead, L'il Abner. By my senior year in high school I had grown to 6'2", which I'm sure was the only requirement to win the role, though I was a stick than at only 150 pounds soaking wet. I was in decent shape having played the strenuous season of water polo just a few months before. I'd also traveled with the Knight Raiders for all of one summer and part of another. Yet I felt terribly wrong for the part and excited to get to play it all at the same time.

That show became a cause for me. I learned all my lines in just a few days. In fact, I knew everyone's lines. The songs were easy, though I probably sang flat. Most young untrained singers do. I'd always sung along with my folk's Frank Sinatra records. My mother even hoped I'd one day be 'the next Frank'.

The show served another purpose. I had no trouble being Stewart while rehearsing and acting in it. Acting provided a ready cover; a facade even better and certainly more fun than sports. I had the body of a leading man and an improving voice to go with it; a high baritone; not quite tenor, not quite bass. It was a classic Broadway leading man voice, at least in sound.

But I'm pretty sure I sang flat.

4

College Guy

Theater became my new place to hide. During the summer between high school and college, I tried out for and won a spot in a local children's theater production of *Bye-Bye Birdie*. This group was far more rounded and complete than our high school. Here I was required to dance! I suppose the only thing I was less qualified to do than athletics was dancing. I was at that time a gangly guy, too tall for my coordination. I must have *reeked* in the role of Albert, though I did enjoy the singing very much. The group was your classic kid's theater group where the audience is made up nearly entirely of families.

Also that summer, I was struck for the first time by the curse of the teenage years; acne. Mine came on with a vengeance shortly after the *Bye-Bye Birdie* run was finished. The group was running two shows that summer and I was in the chorus for *Oliver* as well. During *Oliver*, I looked like someone had shot me with a pellet gun. Red, oozing, and disgusting lesions marked my face. I felt so bad that during that upcoming fall I would find and pay for my own dermatologist. I was so embarrassed to have acne I could not even bring myself to ask my parents to take me in under the insurance.

◆　　　◆　　　◆

Most people apply for university between November and February of their senior year of high school. Being a master of not thinking about things I did not want to think about, I didn't consider what I would do after high school until May of 1977, a mere 1 month before graduation. At that point I did what any senior with no plans would do, I panicked.

Since not only had I not thought of my future, I had not thought of what career or degree program I would pursuer, I made application to San Jose State University's music department. The reason was simple; music was the only thing I really enjoyed doing. Like most music schools, San Jose State required an audition. Auditions are like interviews. The faculty evaluates the student's current abilities and likelihood for success in the chosen field. I skipped that. I just didn't ever call to schedule the audition. My schooling in the art of brass playing was haphazard at best. The most thorough education I'd yet received in how to play brass was in the Knight Raiders, a drum corps. In the 1970s, drum corps was most *seriously* frowned upon as a bullet point on a resume. I'd never had a private lesson (except on piano) and I'd only played first horn in my high school band during my senior year. I'd never played in an orchestra and had no idea what transposition was, let alone how to accomplish it! (Transposition is the art of mentally changing the key of music so that it will fit with the other players. Orchestral horn parts are notorious for requiring transposition skills for reasons too complex to go into.)

In attempting to get into music school through the proverbial back door, I was finally forced to face my deficiencies as a horn player. I knew I sucked. Yet I was willing to be there unless they forced me to leave, though I had no feeling they would. Even at 17 years old I could tell that the school was in the business of processing students through the department and that in the end, they'd want me if for no other reason than that I helped fill their quota.

Not only did I not audition for college, I did not audition for any ensembles either. Symphonic band and orchestra both required auditions with the conductor. I skipped those, too. My first day in orchestra includes perhaps the most embarrassing moment in my career. The conductor was a stern taskmaster who'd refined the 'conductor's glower' to the point of perfection. The first work of the season was the *Roman Carnival Overture* by Hector Berlioz. I'd never heard of either the piece or the composer.

Being a freshman, and an ignoramus, I was assigned the 4th horn part. The 4th part is the lowest, easiest (which is incorrect, but commonly believed), least challenging (also not correct) part in the horn section. However, the upper-classmen assigned the 3rd part failed to show so the maestro stretched out his long index finger and with a slight flick moved me up to third horn.

I'd met none of the other players. I knew no names and no faces.

"Hey," I asked the second horn, "what's it mean when it says 'horn in E'?"

"Jesus Christ," he muttered under his breath.

Dr. Read, the conductor, raised his arms to begin. *The Roman Carnival Overture* begins with a loud flourish, which ends abruptly, leaving a lone horn to sound a clarion tone. The lone horn in that spot is the third horn.

We got to the spot and I froze. I didn't even know we'd gotten there. I didn't know the piece, the tempo, or the key; *nothing*. When the note in front of me was not played, Dr. Read (who'd stopped conducting as he was waiting for me to begin the note) trained his perfected gaze upon me.

Long he looked then said only, "We go back".

Again; *rattle, flourish, articulate*…this time I knew when to play. I was ready, but I could only squeak out a note; the *wrong* note. Horn in 'E' means the player must transpose each note down a half step from what is printed. But I didn't know that. Dr. Read continued to attempt to start the work and after 5 or 6 tries, he finally gave up unable to even look at me.

My lessons began with perhaps the most patient horn teacher a kid could ever hope to get, Dr. William George. He knew very well I'd not auditioned and he never mentioned it. I think he knew I was too embarrassed. He both praised and pushed me and I felt I owed it to him, and myself, to practice. After all, that was why I was there; to become a horn player. Many of the other horn students complained about practice yet also did very little of it. I did my share of bitching but I also paid 'lip service' in the truest sense of the phrase!

◆   ◆   ◆

I kept up with the youth theater group. The winter show was *Once Upon A Mattress*. In that show I was cast in a lead role. I was asked to play the Prince and felt quite good about that. Even then, San Jose was a large town with well over a million people within its borders and surrounding communities, and I was getting lead roles in this prestigious youth theater group! Then I saw the costume drawings for the show and was horrified! The prince was to wear medieval garb of tunic and tights. It was essentially a dress. And a short one at that! My costume was a dark red velvet tunic (mid-thigh) with bright pink tights underneath. The prince was a geek; a mama's boy; a 'fairy', if you will. The plot has him being foisted upon the much more mature and interesting princess, who is tested for the job of marrying said dweeb of a prince by laying on a huge stack of mattresses under which lies a single small pea. If she can feel the pea, she wins the prince. It's an old story. This is the show that made Carol Burnett a household name.

The terror was huge as we arrived at dress rehearsals. I was not the only guy in one of those short tunics, but I was the only guy in pink tights. I both loved it and loathed it. I loved the look and feel but I was terribly worried about what people would think of me and wondered if they'd see me enjoying myself and figure out my horrible secret. There was so little honesty on my part. I could not hide from my own discomfort and the reason for it, but I refused to examine that discomfort even though presented with a golden opportunity. I made my way through the run and in some respects gave my best performances in the company. I played the geek aspect up to the hilt. It was a role that, shall we say, I was born to play.

◆   ◆   ◆

Once in college, I began to have a much better relationship with my parents; especially my mother. She'd risen through the ranks of State Farm from bottom of the pile secretary pool employee in 1972 to a Bodily Injury Claims Adjuster with a company car in 1978. She raised some 8 pay grades in only six years! Throughout my high school years, she was constantly studying course work for accreditations in insurance related knowledge and skills. She earned her Chartered Property and Casualty Underwriters certificate (CPCU) along with other important courses on her own time studying evenings and weekends.

My days were long with school, practicing, musical theater rehearsal and work (local pizza parlor), and I would often arrive home near 11pm when my mother and father were sitting down for a late night brandy. I would join them (but not in the brandy). It was there that I finally got to know my parents. We discussed all the issues of the day, from politics (they were quite conservative Republicans, so of course I was too), to social issues, their insurance work, sales as a career and its relevance to nearly every other job, and any other topic that came up. I loved those times. They were moments when I was treated as an equal, as a valued adult in their lives, though I was still essentially a child. We'd talk till midnight, or later sometimes, then reluctantly I'd head to bed.

With the nearly meteoric rise in my mother's career, my father's was headed in the opposite direction. He'd suffered a heart attack in 1973 and over the course of the five years from 1973 to 1978 he was home off and on as he became increasingly incapacitated with coronary heart disease. In 1977 he had the first of his, in the end, numerous open-heart surgeries. This made him much more available for casual discussions than he'd been when he was the hard-charging insurance salesman or manager. He'd sit in his lawn chair at the edge of the garage with a cigarette, then after he was arm-twisted into quitting, with a cigar, contemplating the world and his place and fate in it. I'd join him when I was home; pulling up a chair and drinking a coke. He loved music and was always eager to talk about it (especially the loud and fast classical pieces). He'd encourage me to dream about the future. We envisioned a career for me teaching and writing for drum corps, playing in orchestras, teaching at a college, and working in the Hollywood studios recording for movies and television. Contrary to the stereotype of the controlling father, my dad's mantra was 'do something you love and the money will follow'. I always loved him for that. It was my mother's position as well, but I always had the feeling she was more cautious about music as a career than he was.

◆   ◆   ◆

Dreams; everyone has them. There were many, many mornings throughout the years I lived with my parents that I would rise, head downstairs, and honestly not know whether they knew all my shameful secrets or not. I dreamt about being a girl, about being a boy dressing like a girl, and about them discovering that and confronting me. Countless mornings I would expect a strong rebuke only to hear the usual 'good morning dear' from my mother, or 'how are you son' from my dad.

Acne was still an off and on struggle. Sometimes the lesions would border on cystic acne; the kind that leaves scars (the results of which I'm quite aware today). Each visit to the doctor would be the same. He would have me lie on his table and he'd warm-soak a big area. Then he'd press and poke to try and drain the lesions. The worst areas were my chin and all around my mouth. The corners of my neck also took a beating.

But with tetracycline, topical solutions, and a diet change (no more free pizza while on break at my pizza parlor job) I was able to feel like I was slightly less of an ogre by the end of my first year of college. In the fall of 1978 I was cast in *Finnian's Rainbow*. I was asked to play Woody, the singing American who would play opposite the best singing (and looking) woman they could find. They chose Denise. Denise was, unbeknownst to me, 23 years old (which was 2 years beyond the upper age limit of the group). She was a veteran of the local theme park singing and dancing shows. Denise was the most beautiful woman I had ever seen. It did not matter if one were speaking of TV, movies, pictures, or anything else. And she was married.

So, knowing going in that there was no hope of having sex with her, I felt relieved. I'd never believed any woman would really be interested in me anyway and it was a relief to have the pressure off. There is a subtle expectation that only someone raised male would understand. It's as if men are expected to 'go after' beautiful women when they have the chance. I did not want to pursue Denise, though I openly flirted with her during rehearsals. Shows are an intimate setting and two people who pretend to be in love often find an infatuation blooming.

The run went fine (though even *I* began to notice that I sang flat, which meant I was probably the last one to know!) and after the final performance ended we were all to stay and strike the set. Striking the set is where you clear everything you've brought into the theater back out again. It is dirty labor which takes hours to finish and can't be started till the show is over. Striking begins immediately after final curtain. We all stayed. When we finished at 2am, Denise informed me she needed a ride home. Of course I said I would be delighted. With that request my sex radar was beeping very loudly. It was obvious through the run and especially during our strike work that she had enjoyed our time together. By asking for a ride she was giving me that undeniable signal that I required to know that I would not be rejected should I make any advances.

We got to my car and before I could say anything *she* was on *me!* We kissed. Weeks of pent up desire came rushing out as we groped and twisted inside my little Gremlin. Soon through touch and body language it became clear she was interested in more, at which point I stopped her.

Looking down, my words difficult to find, I said, "You're married." That was all. She stopped, not looking at me. I went on. "It would not be right of me to be damaging your relationship with your husband."

"You are such a good person, Stewart," she said, "and that's why I'm so attracted to you." I drove her home; all the while she was holding my hand and looking over at me. I truly loved that feeling! Who wouldn't? To be adored? That was better than sex! I felt lifted up in her sight. There were no thoughts of dressing or of feminine things. I was a *MAN* because this beautiful woman wanted me!

I watched her walk to her door where she turned and just looked at me. It was a long look, ten seconds at least, then without a wave she went inside. I was crushed. It's like that *Seinfeld* episode where George does not understand that his date wants him to go to her place to have sex. *"What have I done,"* I thought. I felt I'd betrayed the entire race of man by turning her down. I was deliriously infatuated with her. The pain and agony lasted for weeks but it finally passed.

My near adulterous relations with a married woman convinced me I had done my last musical theater show. I was a French horn major, not a theater major! I needed to get serious about music, about school, and stop fooling around with 'kid stuff'. All told, I'd been in over half a dozen shows including *My Fair Lady, How To Succeed In Business Without Really Trying* and the aforementioned *Finnian's Rainbow.* But then in the winter of 1979 I needed some new activity to completely occupy any free time. That's when an old friend from high school, college, and Knight Raiders asked me to consider joining The Blue Devils Drum and Bugle Corps. This was exactly what I needed: an activity that required 2-3 rehearsals a week 65 miles one way from home plus an all-summer-long commitment. Drum corps would leave no free time for 'perverted' hobbies. I could stay busy; stay focused on positive things, and grow up!

Around that same time, I became acquainted with a San Jose State student. Lana was also a music major at SJSU. I found her quite attractive and she certainly felt the same about me. The interesting thing about our relationship is that is was so passionless. All of my sexual encounters up to that point were marked by a teenage boy's need to 'get off'. Add to that the reinforcement of masculinity that I derived from them and you can perhaps see how obnoxious I was. Lana was a virgin and wished to remain so. I pressured her to acquiesce. Sex was the one sure-fire thing that always made me feel like a guy.

Also, there was the aspect of being 'on the rebound'. Though I'd really not had any relationship with Denise, I had convinced myself I loved her. The loss of that fantasy left a hole which I conveniently filled with Lana.

We spent lots of time together. But in May of 1979 she contacted mononucleosis. She had been having trouble with her mother and did not want to live at home, so I begged my parents to let her move into our home. When I think of this now, I'm ashamed. As a parent it's the last thing I'd allow my child to do with my blessing, yet my parents agreed. Of course, I was not home that summer, but after my return she still occupied the extra bedroom. We did what couples do from time to time right there in my parents home.

My memories of Lana and of our three-year relationship are so painful for me that I have a difficult time remembering them. In fact, my first draft of this account left her and this time out completely. I did not even realize I'd skipped it until I began re-writing.

That fall of 1979 I began to be aware of how dissatisfied I was with our relationship. Perhaps it was having her in the house all the time which prevented me from any dressing at all. Or maybe it was our vastly differing personalities. I was outgoing, confident, and brash. At the time I felt good about that, not being much aware how I'd developed my persona as a cover for truths I was too ashamed to consider.

I felt so *guilty*. Lana was shy, demure, and quiet. In my quiet moments, I knew not only that I did not love her, but also that I was somehow lying to myself about who and what I was. Shame does amazing things to a person. Consider the climactic scene from the recent movie *American Beauty*. The highly repressed homosexual neighbor, believing the Kevin Spacey character is gay, makes a pass. When he's rebuffed, he feels he must kill Spacey lest someone find out he (the neighbor) is gay. When I saw that I felt a strong sense of understanding. Certainly not for murder, but for that feeling of shame and shock at knowing that someone else might know one's secret. For me, that was such a horrible thought; that someone else might know.

I developed a great fear of introspection; a fear of true self-knowledge. I instead engaged in *faux* growth, reading and re-reading the Ayn Rand novels I previously mentioned and having long discussions with my mother about self-reliance, politics, and positive thinking. But true honesty would have led me directly to gender, sex, and desire, and I was so completely horrified at the thought that I was not 'normal' that I could not allow my thinking to go there.

So in November of 1979, as I considered what breaking up with Lana would mean (finding another girl friend; or worse, facing my own issues!), I instead proposed. It was absolutely completely shameful behavior, because I knew at the time that, in my heart, I did not love or desire to marry Lana. She said yes. In our passion, hers genuine, (I must assume, though perhaps she had her own demons from which she ran, thus into my arms?) mine contrived, we created new life.

We both had our dreams. Mine was to play horn professionally. Lana's was to…I did not know then for I don't think she knew herself though she must have dreamt of something. One true fact was that she was not particularly interested in having a baby. Neither one of us could see ourselves as parents at age 20. I convinced her to abort the child. I've thought about this extensively over the years and feel that, though I remain pro-choice, if I'm to burn in hell it will be over that abortion. I cannot speak for Lana, but I can say that since she had lodgings in my parent's home it would have been no great difficulty to house her till the delivery and then put the child up for adoption. But I allowed my selfishness, my shortsightedness, and my California spoiled brat nature to lead me to the opposite choice.

Of course, Lana had it the worst. She was in great pain for nearly a week. I ministered to her as best I could, but I never cut class to care for her or allowed my schedule to be too disrupted over what I recall thinking of as 'her problem'. What a shit I was.

Shortly after that, my mother took me aside (never knowing that we'd aborted her grandchild) and told me it was time for Lana to go. Her presence had depressed me, Mom said. I had not wanted to see it. But once she said it, I felt allowed, and readily agreed that having Lana there was not good for any of us. Lana moved out.

Our relationship limped along until April of 1981 when I finally broke it off. "But I gave myself to you," she cried as I told her of our breakup. She was right. I behaved so poorly, so irresponsibly, and I felt completely terrible about it. But aside from marrying her, whom even I in my deluded nature could not countenance, there was nothing I could say or do that would make anything better. An apology would have been a good start, but as a shallow and callow 21 year old I did not offer one. I've offered up many over the years in my quiet time musings; prayers one might call them, but I've never spoken to her since. When I think of her I fervently hope she's happy.

◆   ◆   ◆

One benefit of being young is that one can forget even the most awful behavior after some short time. By the summer of 1981, I was enthusiastically awaiting my last summer of drum corps. We'd won again in 1980, so I'd been in the 'big leagues' two years and had two championship rings. From the quality of rehearsals for the 1981 show I knew we had the talent and the show to compete for the top slot again. I was right. We had our rocky spots, but in the end we gave it our all. I'm particularly proud of the way the horn and drum lines were more cordial and friendly to one another in 1981, a vast improvement over 1979 and 1980 when the poorly scoring drum line was the target of cruel jokes and snide comments by horn players with overly inflated egos.

We entered championship week in Montreal feeling like we were ready to give the performances of our lives. We did, though we came up short to our intra-state rivals The Santa Clara Vanguard. Second place never felt so good. There is a wonderful feeling a person can get when they know they've done all they can both in preparation and in the moment of performance. We lost to the better group, though some fans disagreed with the judge's choice.

Despite all of my time spent in drum corps with 130 other young people, I was at heart a loner. As I progressed through my last year at San Jose State, I spent more and more time in the practice room. But instead of improving, I quickly slid into a slump. A slump is where a person cannot play their instrument as well as they think they used to or as well as they think they ought to. Slumps are always mental in that although the body is different every day, after some training, one knows how to operate the instrument. So, diminishing abilities are always the mind's way of trying to make one aware of something.

In my case, the most immediate problem was that I knew I had far more to learn in order to play professionally than I could learn in one year, so I began (without really knowing this until much later) to fear failure. I also feared the coming of graduation. I've now seen this in many college seniors. They are about to embark on their careers, so fears abound. In my case, I was not an education major. I was not preparing to, nor did I desire to, teach school. Most music majors graduate with a teaching certificate. They do this either because they desire to teach or as a fall-back career in case they fail in their desire to be performers. Much like during my senior year of high school I chose not to think about the future, focusing instead on trying to play better.

As many people have discovered, when one focuses on a problem one can either solve it, or get what we in the music business call 'the paralysis of analysis'. I continually analyzed my problems, and so became paralyzed and stuck in the poor habits I'd developed. The further the school year progressed the worse I played. By my graduation in May 1982 I was completely frustrated. So to salve my feelings I begged my parents to loan me enough money to go the Aspen Music Festival. I figured that the environment would stimulate me into coming out of my slump.

It did. Aspen is a lovely place and I enjoyed practicing near running streams at the 8000-foot altitude. I also met a lovely lady who seemed to like me very much. This was the pattern I used after Lana. I let them come on to me (very flattering!) then gave in to their advances. I thought nothing about this tactic then, but as I look back; how female that is. I enjoyed being the object of someone else's desire.

Linda was a flute player from rural Minnesota. I resisted her obvious advances for weeks. I was thinking back to how eager I was to be rid of Lana only one year before. I felt I needed to be free for music. Without entanglements I felt I could concentrate better, for by that time I began to realize that it would take me years to become good enough to play professionally.

Perhaps due to a lack of performing opportunities at Aspen or perhaps just due to Linda's persistence (or my own libido?), by the 6th week of the 9-week course she and I were spending every available moment together. Linda was a devout Lutheran so there was no sex, which disappointed me. Since age 11 or so I had believed that manhood was expressed through the sexual act. My father's movie night, his talks to me, and my male body had had his desired effect. I was extremely interested in sex.

Aside from Lana, I had been with only 2 or 3 other girls in high school. I was the first in my clique to 'score' which embarrassed me in that they teased me, but I was at least being teased for exhibiting very male behavior.

It's often been said that a woman should withhold sex from a man until they are married or committed for if he gets what he wants he'll be off to the next conquest. Linda made me wait. We both went home from Aspen with the burden of a 2000-mile relationship on our hands. We wrote some but mostly it was long and costly phone calls. Conversations with lots of silence and lots of 'so, what are *you* thinking,' and other mooney stuff.

After returning from Aspen, I faced the cold reality of adulthood. My parents made it plain; if I was not in school I had to work. A college graduate with a music degree is qualified for little and visions of my new work jargon flooded my mind: *'Would you like fries with that?'* So I asked my Dad to help me get a job selling life and car insurance for Prudential; his employer.

I spent the next three months working sixteen hour days learning the ins and outs of the insurance business. My reward was that Linda came out for a visit in December. She was ready to have sex. I was thrilled, of course, but we also had a great time touring the wine country and seeing the beautiful sights of California.

On one afternoon, we were coming down a winding mountain road and she picked up my wallet which I'd placed in the space in the dash. She flipped it open and rummaged through eventually finding my old picture of Lana. I could feel the cold front even before she said anything.

"Why do you have this picture?"

I'd had a three-year relationship with Lana and although I was glad to be out of it, I had high regard for her and was still carrying much guilt about her pregnancy, abortion, and the way I dumped her. When faced with that question I did what any guy would have done: I lied.

"Oh, it's nothing. I'd just not gotten around to throwing it out."

"Good," she said, tearing it up and throwing it out the window. Things were frosty for an hour or more.

I visited her too, meeting her family and spending time in her apartment. This got her into big trouble with her landlady, who did not approve of girls entertaining overnight guests in her building. Linda ended up being evicted for that!

I left that trip even more convinced than I had been that I loved Linda more than my life and wanted to spend the rest of it with her. I pressed her over the phone in subsequent weeks to expresses similar feelings to mine. We talked openly of marriage. I put in for a transfer with Prudential.

By early May the transfer was approved and I was set to start in the Minneapolis office that July. I called Linda with the good news. She *said* nothing was wrong, but I could tell she was not happy with that news. I sensed cold feet on her part; sensed that this was all happening far too fast. I was still not a Lutheran and was steadfast in my agnosticism.

She called me Memorial Day weekend with the news that we were done. I'd never been so angry or down about a woman before. I canceled my transfer but did not come out of my funk for weeks. It's easy to see now that my guilt over how I'd treated Lana led me to find, or get found, by someone who would dump me. I guess I needed that and so found it.

With the summer free to work and practice I indulged in some thinking. I'd been living with a colleague from work and it was costing me $300 a month for my half of the rent. This illustrates how things have changed in the San Francisco bay area. That nice apartment in east San Jose would now go for over $3000 a month only some 20 years later. I decided I had not really given music my all and would re-dedicate myself to that. My father was particularly supportive and offered to help. He suggested I move back to the family house and pay them $500 a month in rent. He would put that into an account for my master's degree. I jumped at the chance. That fall I started hanging around San Jose State again. I was there not as a student but just as a community musician eager to play in the ensembles. One year of studying with (San Jose Symphony Principal Horn) Wendell Rider had already had a dramatic impact and I was installed as first horn in the band, even though I wasn't enrolled in school.

I also let me eye wander to some of the lovely ladies there in the group. I began to get to know Laurie; a quiet, shy, and demure woman. She was able to allow me to feel the man I thought I should be while also being extremely easy to be with.

During that fall of seeing Laurie I prepared to audition by tape at 5 colleges for masters programs. I thought the most accurate representation of my playing would come from a live performance so I prepared a recital of varied works. On December 23, 1983, I gave that concert and it was a quantum leap in excellence from anything I'd done up to then. For the 6 weeks leading up to the concert I was at the university 6-7 days a week for 2 or more hours per night practicing that music. I had 6-8 hours of rehearsal with my pianist. I spared no expense and consequently felt that I had every right to expect excellence.

This is how life works. If you want to be good at something, you must decide that you will do whatever it takes—*whatever*—to succeed. I don't mean killing or stepping on others. That is the way to hell. But the key is the willingness to do anything in your power to succeed. I practiced at every opportunity. I had my horn with me in my car at all times. If I had a half hour between business appointments, I got out the horn and played right there on the street. Every morning when I drove to the office, I sat in the parking lot and practiced for a half hour or more. Lunch was a quick, quick bite, and then practice. As I drove in the awful (even then) traffic of what was then beginning to be called Silicon Valley, I went through my recital music in my head. I thought of the phrasing I wanted and sang my parts *on pitch*.

I once heard it said that if you want to be an expert at something, you must put in 10,000 hours before you'll succeed. In 1982 I was perhaps approaching the 4000-hour mark; the beginnings of competence.

After the concert, I knew it had gone well and pictures from that night show me to be very pleased with myself. Gone were any feelings of inadequacy and inferiority. I played well, I was seeing a lovely woman who desired me, and I was about to apply to colleges which would (I hoped) all beg me to come. Around this time feelings of competence were the best antidote to feminine feelings. This period of time from breaking up with Linda to moving to Cincinnati represents one of the longest stretches I remember being relatively free of gender conflict. A short one-year, but it still has in my memory more life packed into it than many other periods of time.

I suppose this was the last gasp of adolescence; the last time in my life when I would feel so invincible. We all grow up eventually and learn of the hardships of life. For a relatively pampered California boy, my teens were lasting until my mid 20's. By my observations that was about average for the Bay Area. Halcyon days; my memory frames them in a sunny glow.

Even so, I can also recall moments of blue when I'd contemplate my unthinkable dilemma. The mind has amazing ways to maintain locked doors and closets. In my teens, whenever the gender issue became overwhelming, I would dress, masturbate, feel immensely guilty, and actually believe it would never happen again; that I was finally free of it. In my early twenties, and even during those halcyon days, I could no longer believe I would be rid of it. I knew that if I allowed myself to even *think* of it I would do it. The solution was time management: to be so busy that there was no alone time; no personal relaxation time. My unacknowledged goal was to be so busy as to not have the opportunity for the thoughts to even cross my mind.

I spent large blocks of time with girlfriends, I practiced an enormous amount, I worked jobs at all times through college, I had participated in a 24 hour a day activity during the summers (drum corps), and if there was nothing else I watched television. The idiot box was great for telling my brain what to think about.

Stewart the solitary model builder, the bookworm, the soft and feeling person; I had years of practice in covering that person with a veneer of the male I thought I was supposed to be. From surviving bullies, to family ridicule, to explicit descriptions of the behavior of males; at 24 I was firm in my role. I knew how to treat women (I thought) and how to engage in a conversation. I knew how to look a person in the eye and talk to them. I'd had 18 months of sales experience where if you cannot convince someone that you're honest you don't earn your living. I was (mostly) confident that I was just a regular guy.

I recall one particular night. I'd gone to an empty field near my house to practice. I did this because I knew that my mother did not like to hear the horn in the house, as it was quite loud no matter what I did. So I'd only practice at home if she was away. It was dusk and I could see the mountains in the distance, the 4000 foot peak of Mt. Hamilton with Lick observatory shining in the sunset at the top, and I knew; I just *knew*: I would be leaving California forever by the end of the summer of 1984. I could hardly wait. At that point I had heard nothing from the graduate schools to which I'd applied, I only knew I had applied and that I *would* be leaving.

By March, all the schools responded as I'd expected: accepted. However, only The University of Cincinnati offered me a deal I could not refuse: a scholarship covering all tuition for two years. I signed, and was sealed and delivered. I was moving to Cincinnati.

Being so focused on goals other than selling insurance, my work results began to show the lack of attention. I knew I had become a liability to the company by February of 1984. I went to my boss and offered my resignation.

He sat me down and said, "Listen, you've just broken a good quarter (this meant that in the previous 13 weeks I'd done very well selling lots of policies, hence I had a big fat paycheck coming for the next quarter of a year which represented my own hard work) why don't you stick around and collect that while you service all of your accounts. I won't expect you to sell too much but I will expect you to answer anyone's complaints. Deal?"

How can one turn down the opportunity to clear $600 a week and only have to show up a few hours a week? I agreed, clear of conscience that I had offered to do the right thing and quit once I knew I could/would not do the job any more.

Six weeks into that quarter, we got a new district manager. On his first day in his first hour he called me into his office. My boss, Jeff, went with me for he knew what was coming as much as I did.

The boss said, "Young man, when was the last time you sold a policy?"

"Six weeks ago," I replied.

"You're worthless and lazy. You're fired. Clean out your desk and be gone in half an hour." Jeff tried to explain our deal, but the new guy just cut him right off.

Jeff wanted to talk right after the firing and I said, "Listen, I got six weeks I would not have. I thank you for that. You perhaps did more than you should have." After 18 months of sales, I was back into the world of minimum wage and take what you can get.

For the six months between my firing from Prudential and leaving for Cincinnati in mid-August I worked a variety of jobs, mostly being a driver for a wheel distributor and as a telemarketer (*what fun!*). I had about $5000 saved due to my father's deal and I did not want to dip into that. He said I did not have to pay rent to the savings anymore once I was fired from Prudential so the money I made went to the regular expenses such as gas, insurance, eating out, and other stuff.

Laurie agreed to accompany me on the drive out east so we took a huge detour and went to Disneyworld, followed by the Drum Corps International Championships which were in Atlanta. We had a great time until I had to take her to the airport in Atlanta for her flight home. We both knew it was the end of our relationship. We wrote and saw each other again for a few days the following summer, but we knew it was over.

I killed that relationship. I'd been through a 2 year relationship with Lana that I could not wait to leave, fell over my head for Linda in Minnesota and could not believe she dumped me, and had a brief but ultimately sad relationship with perhaps the best person I'd ever known, Laurie. But I was convinced I needed space to get down to the work of becoming the horn player I thought I could be.

In the rush of such changes, in my secret heart, I also hoped I'd be leaving behind my childhood perversion, my guilty secret. Now that I was on my way to professionalism, I was even more determined be the man I'd set out to become.

But huge changes in life have a way of making you see who you really are. New cities and new environments afford the opportunity to re-set the path of life; to engage with people in a more open and honest way. But I did not like questions about myself. I wanted *certainty*. I knew absolutely nobody in Cincinnati. So I decided to show them the person I thought I should be; the person I thought I was.

5

A New Life—Cincinnati

I moved into the high-rise graduate student dorm, Scioto Hall, in August of 1984. With four weeks until school began I got down to work by getting a job at the local 7-11. I was fortunate to work with and for some really great people while there so scheduling was easy. I practiced daily for 3-5 hours which still left me with time on my hands.

I vividly remember during my first few weeks in Cincinnati pacing my one room apartment being torn apart by gender issues. I could not bring myself to do something to take my mind off it. Masturbation put down the worst of it for a time, but I knew that was not a permanent solution to the problem. While I wished to dress and look like a woman I was ashamed and embarrassed by the sexual connection between the two.

The young male body is a sex machine. It is designed to impregnate women and cast its seed throughout the land. In my research on 'dressing' as I called it then, it's said the classic symptom of a transvestite is that he dresses when the stress level gets too high. This description *seemed* to fit me, and once I'd found it (whenever I could allow myself to think about it at all) I labeled myself a transvestite. However, other aspects of the transvestite model did not fit me. Cross dressers (as they prefer to be called) also enjoy normal sexual relations with their wives or girlfriends and have no desire to become women. They simply want to look like women from time to time. None of those last descriptions fit me at all, especially the descriptions of sex.

Normal sexual relations consist, I've been told, of people desiring each other. I desired orgasm and a confirmation of my male identity. However, I quickly got comfortable with a woman and sex faded from the picture. This was the pattern I would live with until my transition. I used sex as a tool to confirm an identity, *a persona,* for myself. In more casual and uncommitted relationships that decrease of desire often became a non issue due to the ending of the relationship.

My moments of lucidity and honesty about this issue were very few indeed in 1984. When I dressed I wanted to be a woman, but I felt so awful about feeling that way in the first place it would be another six years before I allowed myself to completely dress for the first time since childhood.

My initial loneliness and confusion after moving to Cincinnati was eased with the start of the school term. Lessons were begun, as well as classes and auditions for the orchestra. Unlike my undergraduate tactic of sneaking in the back door, the Cincinnati College-Conservatory of Music was a big time school so I had to actually take the auditions in order to play in any groups. I had no idea how good or bad the groups were, I just went in and played my best. I was very pleased when I saw the result: I'd made it into the top ensemble.

The first rehearsal was an unforgettable experience. I could not help smiling as I heard a sound and a precision I'd only ever heard from recordings of professionals. This orchestra could play! And I was in it! I was the fifth player which meant that I assisted the first horn player, a junior undergraduate, but an exceedingly good player. But I did not see that low position as a comedown at all, I was just happy to be there.

I soon met a wonderful woman; one might call her a girl as she was barely 20. We enjoyed some easy camaraderie and casual flirting. Within a few weeks we were spending our nights together, too. Lena was one of those women who know exactly the effect they have on men and make it happen as often as possible. I played my usual game of flirting and being friendly but never making any advances. I waited for her. I cannot remember exactly how we ended up in her bed but it was probably after drinking at the local bar where a number of us would go after rehearsals and concerts.

With the attentions of Lena I was once again free of the need to think of or wear women's clothes. We explored every possible sexual position and technique. After a few months she tired of me and that was that. I was not so gracious. I displayed a horrible immaturity by playing the jilted lover. Though I grew from that experience, I hate to look back and see myself as I really was.

During that first year, I met many people and agreed to share an apartment with two guys for the following year. We moved in August and the closeness of that prevented me from dressing. Ah! The value of roommates; they helped keep me in line. Friends, practice and work, those were the tasks for each day, but not necessarily in that order!

I began a period of intense wild oat sowing. I was the classic bad boy; love 'em and leave 'em. It was terrible behavior. In a way, I backed into that lifestyle. I was not the type of person who could approach a woman and get what I wanted. So I played the 'I don't need anyone' game, and for a year never failed to be alone for long. After feeling used one woman told me off in no uncertain terms; a tongue-lashing I'll never forget (no pun intended). As I look back I've asked myself what I was seeking: a mate? Sex? What? I now know: it was proof. I needed proof that I was a guy and my father had taught me well. I needed to continually prove to *myself* that my definition of being a man was right: men are people who have sex with women.

It was around this time that my mind began to think that since I could not shake the thought of myself as a woman I must be gay. I knew a number of gay guys but could not bring myself to get anything going with them. I was not attracted to them, though when I was honest, the thought of being with a man was definitely present. All through this time my thoughts of dressing and of being a woman were held way back in my mental closet. When I thought of them at all it was pure agony and I shut them back in their locked box as quickly as I could.

◆   ◆   ◆

By the second year in Cincinnati, I lost a job at a church that had paid me $200 a month for little to no work. As a result, I dropped out of the master's program to work full time at the 7-11. I did continue to take lessons and play in the orchestra. An interesting note here: I was not aware at all that doing so might be wrong or inappropriate. I wanted to play in an orchestra, so why shouldn't I? But now that I look back, I was paying nothing for school nor was I any longer on scholarship. I was more of a community player that second year, yet I played in the top orchestra taking a spot that an enrolled student might have gotten had I not been there. This is a great example of male privilege. Male privilege is where advantages and opportunities come one's way when equally qualified and talented women do not get them. It's also a state of mind in people raised male. They carry a sense of entitlement with them. It's not really even a decision. It's a mental *fait accompli*. In the orchestra they were happy to have me at that time, and I was quite happy to be there. Of course, the 'courtesies' extended to me also disenfranchised younger male students as well.

A more grievous example of my blindness to male privilege happened in that second year. Our first horn player was taking lessons on the side with Dale Clevenger, first horn of the Chicago Symphony. Greg (our first horn player) asked me to cover his part for the next day's rehearsal, as he had a lesson in Chicago. He felt if he asked to be excused they'd say no and lower his grade, so he planned on calling in sick. The plan was that he would say he called me and asked me to play first just that morning. We would then shuffle the assistant first player over to second, which was actually my assigned part. Protocol stipulates that the assistant move up; it was, after all, her job to know the first horn part. But I happily circumvented the chain of command to facilitate my own 'career'. And Greg knew just what to say to me to get me to do it.

"I'm worried that if Ann steps up, the conductor will not like the way she plays it and be mad at me."

So I agreed to his plan. I feel bad to this day for what I did to Ann. She's gone on to a fine career, including regularly substituting with the New York Philharmonic. But my part in that incident left a lasting impression on both of us. From then on she hated me; virulently. And I've regretted my poor conduct. Naturally, I did not play well that day. Truly ultimate justice.

One outstanding example of the level of playing at CCM in the 80s was when H. Teri Murai, the conductor of the second orchestra at CCM, came over to Philharmonia (the top orchestra at CCM at that time) to prepare and conduct a performance of Shostakovich's Symphony No. 4. This great Russian (really Soviet) composer had been the darling of the state until the late 1930s, when Stalin turned on him. The 4th symphony was written just before that attack, and Shostakovich pulled it from public performance before it could be criticized. Cultural attacks from Stalin could prove deadly as artists who did not please the state often ended up dead and Shostakovich well knew this. It's one of the reasons his music became more unpopular with the authorities; they heard the double meanings in his music, including the sarcastic and 'formalist' (their term, meaning following the conventions of 20th century Western music; a sin in the Soviet Union) traits. Shostakovich had been an ardent communist in the early days of the revolution, but the bloom was soon off the rose as he saw people being repressed and persecuted for speech, deed, and often for mere thought. These changes in the regime, mostly heralded in by Stalin, and Shostakovich's feelings about them, caused an audible reaction in his art.

None of us at CCM in the 80s knew much of Shostakovich's music other than his wildly popular 5th symphony, and were ignorant of the story behind his music. Teri taught us the story, the reasons why he wrote what he wrote, but we continued to balk and whine. Finally, during the dress rehearsal, one of those magical moments that musicians live for began to happen: we all started to *get it*. The meanings became visible through the fog of the notes. We stepped through the technique required to perform the music to just *be* the music. The next night in the performance we were like dogs with a really good bone; single minded, relentless, and thoroughly committed. It remains to this day one of the finest musical performances of my career; not so much because I played well, though I did, but because of the total group focus. It was my first taste of that kind of feeling since leaving drum corps (where that type of feeling is common and the whole point) in 1981.

◆   ◆   ◆

Living with two men made it difficult to get some privacy. My feminine wardrobe was nil. I'd occasionally buy some pantyhose using a 'clever' way to buy them without facing down the clerk. I'd make a shopping list for the grocery store and add the pantyhose to the list. Then I'd make a big deal out of holding the list in front of me while I scanned the display and checked the packaging 'to be sure I've got what she wants'. This little game allowed me to face purchasing some things. I also used the tried and true 'buying a gift for my girlfriend' act at clothing stores, but since I knew I'd probably throw the stuff away after a few episodes, I could not bring myself to spend the money that often.

Billy and Reb (my roommates) were seldom there, but I never knew when they'd come home. I had a room with a deadbolt so I would indulge, but where would I go? I was increasingly disgusted at being segregated from the world. I believe this was the gender dysphoria, the tearing of identity, growing in intensity and strength. I needed to admit to the truth, but I was still too ashamed to allow that it was in fact truth at all. I still had a huge fear of this issue; that someone would know this about me. I could not stop the occasional dressing, and I also could not stop myself from thinking about it.

My 'bad boy' behavior led me into a relationship with a pianist. I'd hired her to be my musical partner on a recital and she sent me those unmistakable signals after our work ended. We spent time together, and I believe enjoyed each other's company. After a couple of months, she came to me and to say she was not going to be seeing me any longer.

Then she said something I've always remembered, for it resonated with me in a way I was, at the time, not willing to examine. She said, "I hope you find what you're looking for."

Indeed. Shortly thereafter, late in that my second year in Cincinnati, the orchestra was scheduled to play *The Love For Three Oranges*. This funny opera by Prokofiev is scored for full orchestra and included parts for six horns, so we brought in 2 extra players from the horn studios. One was a woman I'd never seen before, though I'd heard of her. Wendy was working on a master's degree in German and already had bachelor's degrees in music and German. She was one of the extras and I was quite taken with her. I knew I was tiring of the 'Don Juan' game I'd been playing but since I was not ready to be honest with myself, I needed another woman in my life to help me avoid the painful self examination of which I was so desperately in need.

The pattern I'd established of noticing their interest, returning that interest, spending some time together, waiting for the unmistakable signal that they'd like to be closer, and having sex was still rooted in my psyche. Wendy and I flirted throughout the production. After the run of performances, we met at the cast party and talked…and talked. The next day we spent lots of time together and within a couple of weeks we were in bed.

That same month of May 1986 was a big one for both Wendy and me. We were both scheduled to audition for the Dayton Philharmonic, a small budget regional orchestra, but a paying orchestra job nonetheless. We'd both been preparing diligently and along with about a dozen other area horn players went to Dayton to give it our best shot. When all was said and done, I was asked to join the orchestra as the new fourth horn. I later learned that one of the Co-Principal Horn players, whom I had previously met at CCM, believed I had treated him poorly and he was not in favor of hiring me even though I'd won the blind audition. Then the other Co-Principal spoke up. It turned out she'd been in a long simmering feud of sorts with that other player.

She said to her colleague, "You know, people change. You've changed." Her willingness to speak up put the job in my lap.

Shortly after winning the Dayton job the lease on my apartment expired. I'd accepted a summer chamber music festival offer and was due to leave for Maine in late June. I was not about to rent another apartment for three weeks, so I'd planned to throw my sleeping bag into the horn room each night. The horn room was a small practice room given over to the storage of each hornist's instrument. Activity there was over by 11pm so I figured I could sleep there without disturbing anyone.

After one night, Ann, who I'd so wrongly fouled, went to the Dean to complain about the 'vagrant' in the horn room and the smell (we never think we smell, but to others…*whew*). I was called in to speak with Lowell, my teacher, who was nearly beside himself with laughter. He found the situation quite amusing. I did too, but the word was clear; no more sleeping in the horn room. I needed a place to stay. I called Wendy.

It turned out that she was leaving for Germany in late August for a year of study. She won that tuition free year for outstanding accomplishments in the Foreign Language department. However, she already owned a home; a duplex at that. She had a tenant in the upstairs apartment whose rent covered the mortgage. I'd never known such a competent and self-assured woman. We made an arrangement. She swears to this day that my attraction to her was greed; that I wanted an inexpensive place to live. The agreement was I would pay $100 a month while she was gone, and I would pay all her bills out of the rent as well as look after her home.

I'd never had a relationship quite like the one I had with Wendy. Being with Lana was similar, but she was so mild and acquiescent that the only similarity was my desire to be out of the relationship. However, I was not too consciously aware of this. I had a huge ability to lie to myself. I was, in essence, doing it continually in order to not be continually bothered by gender and my troubling inner visions of myself. So I told myself I enjoyed being with Wendy and hoped that simply saying it would make it so.

While at the chamber music camp in Maine, I met a number of people. One was a young violinist who was quite attracted to me. A part of me wanted to reciprocate, but on the whole I was quite relieved to be able to tell her I was taken. I felt myself a person of at least some honor, though my sexual behavior displayed over the previous year would lead one to think otherwise.

After my return, Wendy and I had only a few days before she was to leave for Germany. These were stressful and awkward. We had little initial compatibility. We were not sexually turned on by each other, at least I was not by her, and we had wildly diverging politics. I was an Ayn Randian style capitalist since high school and she was what most classical musicians are: a liberal democrat. Part of my ability to pass, to stay sane as Stewart, was to be rigid about many things. Politics was one.

Oh how I loved Ayn Rand's books! Her characters, or should I say her *male* characters, had all that I thought a person would aspire to be: They were strong, sure of themselves, and curiously unconcerned about what other people thought of them. While I now know that I was completely under the spell of the opinions of others, my heroes, my fictional role models, were anything but! Rand's novels are filled with black/white comparisons. Good is great and bad is so bad, so obviously wrong, that no one could disagree. I must have read *Atlas Shrugged*, her magnum opus and most controversial book, at least a dozen times. I could never get enough of the triumphs of John Galt, Hank Reardon, and Francisco D'Anconia. What did I get out of this? I was able to reinforce my own version of manhood. 'Be a man like Hank Reardon is a man'. These characters helped me, but only to a point.

Since they were fictional constructs, I became much like fiction. Sure, I was dedicated to learning to play the horn. I was honest (about legal things, obviously not about myself!) and persistent in my zeal to become a professional musician. However my closed mindedness made me stuck.

In 1986, I was still very much hiding from myself. The knowledge of who I really am was just beginning to break over me and I wanted nothing to do with it. I wanted Reardon and Galt, not...*me*. There is an oft-repeated question among transsexuals, a complete fantasy, but interesting: 'If you could take a pill and forevermore feel like a 'normal' man, would you?' At that time, I most definitely would have. I hated this aspect of myself. That is often at the center of the gender syndrome sufferer's agony; self hate. I knew there was much to like, yet I longed for these feelings, these desires, to disappear. I wanted to *want* to fuck like so many of the other guys I knew. I tried so hard, too hard really, to be like them.

When I met Wendy and began that relationship, I was beginning to tire of the struggle. Sexual conquest was no longer the drug that could relieve me of my pain. I needed to be healed; I needed to be a regular guy From my earliest days with this situation as a 4 and 5 year old kid, I could see a growing awareness of this. All along the way I thought about it as little as I possibly could. By age 27 I was far too aware of what I called my 'perversions'. But even at 27 I would not think further. I just could not face the issue head-on. I needed to find a cure. Wendy seemed to present an excellent cure. I could be involved with her and she would be away in a different country.

I was due to return to the master's program at CCM in the fall of '86. This was made possible in large part by my rental manager/low rent arrangement with Wendy. I could get by on less money by living there. With her out of the country I could feel tied up, but not feel that pressing need to be involved sexually. Most crucial perhaps was that I was not honest with myself about the fact that I did not much enjoy sex.

I went to Germany at Christmastime 1986 to visit Wendy. She was gracious and kind showing me many wonderful places. I was rude, not affectionate, and quite a poor traveling companion. When I returned from Germany in January 1987, I felt quite relieved. I've since come to understand that I'm not a big fan of travel. I miss my home while I'm away and greatly look forward to returning. At that time, I was eager to get back to school, back to practicing on my regular schedule and back to my exciting new job in the Dayton Philharmonic. I also continued to work at United Dairy Farmers, a convenience store chain based in Cincinnati, where I usually covered the midnight shifts on weekends.

◆   ◆   ◆

That first year as a (semi) professional player taught me a great deal about my deficiencies in concentration. While I was quite capable, especially as I prepared my parts at home, once I got on the job my mind seemed to wander. I would eagerly follow the thread of stray thoughts as they floated across my consciousness like so much tree cotton on a warm June day. Each concert would leave me angry at myself for doing any number of amateur things: miscounting rests, playing wrong dynamics, not matching the other horn players, playing out of tune with the section, and generally being a distraction to all around me. At least that is how I remember that first season. I subsequently was asked, despite my weaknesses, to stay on and I received the coveted tenure, which meant they felt I was qualified to be a regular member of the orchestra.

My last two quarters at CCM contained the only significant experiences of playing orchestral first horn prior to 1990. With the departure of Greg (a more experienced student) to full time horn employment, I became the conductor's choice for the first chair. I recall that in 1984, my first year at CCM, another horn graduate horn student asked me if I thought I was cut out to play principal horn. I answered that I thought I had the temperament for it. He did all he could to hide his incredulity and shock at the answer, though he failed. I've since learned that I do have a very different personality from the classic model of a first chair orchestral brass player. The usual type is extremely confident. The old saying, 'their shit don't stink' will always come to mind. This is actually a very helpful mental state. Like a great athlete, errors can soon be forgotten, or even re-interpreted as being merely 'quirks'. My tendency is to be extremely self-critical, often to the point of physical revulsion. I'm sure much of it has its roots in my gender confusion. However, the benefit is that I've experienced a very steep learning curve. I've been able to greatly improve my skills over the years. As with any skilled and difficult art, improvement is not a straight line but a series of tangents followed in response to current disasters. Those two quarters of playing first horn helped me develop a better working method for quality improvements.

While I was gaining status, strength, and confidence in my horn playing ability, my personal life was like quicksand under my feet. I suppose living alone was beneficial in that I did not have to *be* with someone, but at the same time it allowed all my cross gender feelings to surface much easier than when I was on conquest or tied down in a daily relationship. As was my pattern, gender confusion brought out the need to escape from my own private hell by getting into a new relationship. Fortunately, the person I chose was far more mature than me and rebuffed my flirtatious advances citing my existing relationship with Wendy.

My cross-dressing continued at irregular intervals. Living alone afforded one benefit I'd not had since first moving to Cincinnati; the freedom to dress and remain at ease in the clothes. The usual pattern was that I was so horrified and ashamed I could not relax and just exist. The dressing would also include a largely unwelcome flood of sexual desire. I became increasingly repulsed by the needs of my body. It seemed to have a mind of its own, reacting to clothing and the cross gender feelings in what I considered inappropriate ways. When I would give in to dressing, I would insist that I remain clothed for a 'significant' period, an hour or more, in order to force my body to stop responding sexually. I would read, watch television, or even practice my horn.

The sexual aspects of this condition are, in my opinion, incidental to the identity issues. In the 80's, scholarly experts were writing that *any* sexual excitement concomitant with dressing was irrefutable evidence that the person was nothing more than a fetishistic cross-dresser. However, fetish implies that the article is necessary for sexual excitement. That was not the case with me. But those 'experts' were *positive: anyone* sexually excited when thinking of, or actually cross-dressing, was a transvestite. When I first read this in the late 80s I was actually relieved. A transvestite simply suffered from a sexual perversion. They were still 'regular guys' most of the time.

But a larger 'chicken and egg' type question here is begged: Are transsexuals experiencing sexual desire as a byproduct of the dressing or is the dressing *required* to experience sexual feeling? In my case, my shame over the entire issue kept me from delving into the subject very deeply. But I've since come to believe that it's far more complicated than even that simplistic 'chicken and egg' question implies. The human male body is designed for sex. It is hormonally hard wired to become aroused and ready to mate at very short notice. During puberty the sexual aspects of the male body are even more pronounced. For me it often took little more than thought to cause an erection; thoughts of women (or men), of the sex act, or of dressing, let alone the actual donning of clothing.

In April of 1987, Wendy decided to return early from Germany. She'd been accepted for the fall class of graduate horn study at CCM, and knowing what course she would pursue for the foreseeable future was eager to start on that path. Upon arrival at home she asked me to move out as soon as possible. My distance and waffling relationship with her was unacceptable. She was eager to meet someone who would truly like her and love her for herself. I believe she sensed, far more than I was able to see myself, that I was using her to hide.

From that point forward Wendy and I maintained a 'come here/go away' type of relationship. With each of us lonely and still generally enjoying the company of the other, we would occasionally meet for coffee or spend evenings together. Wendy's is one of the most brilliant minds with which I've ever had the pleasure of spending time, and by the spring of 1988 she and I were as involved as we had been previously except for living in separate homes. I was due to go to Nashville for that summer to work in an amusement park (now gone) called *Opryland*. That park specialized in not only rides but live shows, all with live musicians to accompany. They hired quite a number of great players from all over the country, but only one horn player. I felt fortunate to get the work.

In May of '88, a few weeks before I was to leave, I decided that I'd had enough of the crazy dance with Wendy and chose to break it off for good. I went to meet her. I'd learned over the years to be quite cold when involved in a stressful emotional event. My childhood defense against my confusion was to shut off all emotion and I generally lived my life that way. Now with a break-up impending, I pushed down my emotions even further. I told her, bluntly and quickly, that I never wanted to see her again. I recall that she smirked. Something I came to see much more in future years. It was as if she knew me better than I knew myself and was saying, 'that's what you say now, but you'll be back'.

I felt great…for a few moments. After the goodbye I got in my car to go for a drive, usually a relaxing thing for me at the time. Within three miles, I was crying in wracking sobs and a flood of tears. I kept driving.

I yelled to myself out-loud, "What is the matter with you! You've got what you wanted. You're free of Wendy now; free to pursue your dreams!" But I only cried harder and harder. There was a truth in there struggling to get out. I've replayed this scene many times, for it cast a die for my future that I'll live with the rest of my life. It's my belief that faced with a choice to be honest with myself, I chose instead to retreat again into the familiarity of the closet. Of course, I'd never called it a closet. That would have lead to associations I was not able to entertain.

After over an hour of crying and driving (probably the ultimate in 'distracted driving') I decided that what I needed was not less Wendy but more. I decided I would ask her to marry me. Ridiculous, you say? Yes, it was. But that's the extent to which I was willing to go to avoid facing my gender issues. I'd never connected the dots of all my relationships before, to see what kind of picture they made, but had I done so then I would have realized that Wendy would be the third proposal I'd made in eight years. There'd been three women I'd been eager to marry. One I ran from (Lana), one ran from me (Linda), and then there was Wendy. If I had not been so focused on moving to Cincinnati for graduate school I knew I would have proposed to Laurie as well. So that really made 4!

I arrived back at her house having only shortly before told her I never wanted to see her again. I did not care if she could tell I'd been crying. I wanted to ask her my question. I don't recall how much preface I gave. Something like, 'I've been doing a lot of thinking....' and other crap like that. And then I asked her.

She laughed. Who wouldn't? It was a completely ridiculous proposal. She refused to even entertain the question, and laughing turned around and went inside.

Over the next few weeks we saw each other more and more and eventually ended up in bed. With our reconciliation, my sexual desire for her rose dramatically. I took this as a sign that I'd done the right thing. I was, after all, becoming a mature adult man and putting all that craziness behind me.

I left for Nashville on the kind of emotional high that only people in love can have. But for me, it was far better. I was not only convinced I was in love, but proud of myself for overcoming my 'perversions'. Wendy had still not said yes or no. Rather, we maintained a loose affiliation; conversational, sexual, and horn related. Then after three weeks in Nashville, Wendy called with some news. She was pregnant and due to deliver in February of 1989. I was thrilled for not only did it solidly affirm my manhood but more closely bound her to me.

My living arrangements in Nashville were interesting. I rented a room in a boarding house. I'd never done that previously and never have since. In the basement with me there was only one other tenant, so I had a decent amount of privacy. Almost immediately upon settling in to my room, my gender issues began to return. I thought of dressing as well as an added stress, I thought of appearing as a woman in public. This was a new and distressing development! Previously, I'd only imagined myself dressed. I'd not thought about going public.

I resisted. But I've come to understand that what we resist persists. It seemed that my resistance only intensified my desire. I decided I'd give in, but just a little. I used my 'works every time' method for buying pantyhose and purchased two pair. Then, in for a penny in for a pound, I decided that I could go out wearing them underneath my shorts. Now I was never, *ever*, mistaken for female after the age of 3 or so (if I had ever been). I had never in my life gone out of the house dressed in any way. But then, all of a sudden (after proposing to Wendy), I had a huge need to take a walk wearing pantyhose! Nashville may be a very cool town but it's still the south. There were numerous young guys who drove their souped-up cars around the neighborhood. I did make one concession to safety: I walked at night. But the hose had sheen so whenever a car would come, I'd duck behind bushes, cars, fences, whatever I could find. There were no streetlights, so the only lights I had to worry about were the headlights.

I recall thinking that I needed to 'see what it was like' to do that. I hoped that by taking that chance I would cure myself. There was no sexual component. In fact I was mostly *terrified*. My breathing was shallow and fast for the entire walk. Upon arriving home again I carefully scoped out the basement to be sure Charlie was nowhere near. I got to my room and changed without being discovered.

But from that day forward Charlie gave me a wide berth. He said nearly nothing whereas we'd been at least cordial before. A few times he let loose with a stream of religious condemnations that truly shocked me. It must have been my foolish neighborhood trek. Either that or he was offended by Wendy's occasional visits.

So my first foray into the world while admitting and showing a bare minimum of my condition came off without being arrested or beaten to a bloody pulp. I tried very hard to not think of it at all. This was the precipice I walked: to know something, but to not see it, admit it, act on it, or acknowledge it in any way.

It is interesting that only after the strong possibility that I would soon be married that I found the need to dress in public overwhelming. I previously mentioned dissociation. These types of things were the epitome of dissociative activities though I fully remembered them. They constituted a form of acting out. I was unwilling to examine why I needed to act out in this way let alone examine the possible consequences to the marriage I'd proposed or the baby I'd helped create.

The consequences of my choice were fast beginning to catch up with me, that choice made a few months before during a crying fit while driving to continue to closet my true self. The harmful effects on my mental health, which would eleven years later nearly claim my life as but another payment due had already for years worked their black magic on my mind.

Was it just shame? I was certainly raised to believe that 'good' people worked, were heterosexual, voted, and just generally fit it with the rest of the 'regular' people that lived in the U.S. Whenever variant types were shown in the media, I can recall my parents, my father especially, commenting on their freakish nature.

It was around this time that I began to understand that they the way I was raised had some meaning. My parents had played some role, though it was an unstudied subject in 1988. Retrospect can be a wonderful thing but it is inherently flawed. The sin of rewriting history is ever present and all too likely. In my search for myself I've been wary of that to the point of not looking closely enough. In the context of 1988, I can safely say that I loved my parents but also feared their condemnation. My own sense, in 1988, of being ashamed was limited to my gender issues which were highly compartmentalized.

The reality of what happened to my sister was but one un-studied conflict in my life. Michelle, the wonderful therapist I would meet in the summer of 1999, often asked me to imagine how a young person might feel while growing up to observe the things my brother and I observed happening to our sister. I had to admit that the fear of it happening to me was probably there. But I must also remain honest: I have no memory of being *overtly* afraid of being thrown out of the house. My parents were steadfast in declaring their love for my brother and me. But logic would dictate that they also, at some point, loved our sister too. That love then turned into extremely 'tough' love. My brother and I were not privileged to know the details of why our sister was treated in the manner she was. We were only told vague things like drugs and rule infractions.

My need to cross dress certainly would fall under the heading of rule infractions in my young mind. By 1988, I began to see that I was largely tied in knots to please my parents. I can recall thinking that for me to tell them I was engaged would really please them, even with the pregnancy. They had at that point only two grandchildren. The soon to be born child would be their third.

From the day I heard the news from Wendy, I knew the baby would be a girl. I don't know how I knew, except that the idea of a young male child in my life just could not, *would not,* fit with my visions. In the emotional desert of my youth there was only one thing that could move me. My parents were big fans of Frank Sinatra and they owned three of his records. One contained the long (7-8 minutes; not radio length at all) 'Soliloquy' from *Carousel.* I loved that number! Actually I loved the way Sinatra could caress a phrase, and to this day he is still one of my models of musical phrasing. 'Soliloquy' is a song where the thief and soon to be father, Billy, contemplates life as a father and how he'll feel about that. It's a song not about love of a girl or boy, but one of a *pure* love, a love of one's child. I have no great Freudian insight as to why as a 12 year-old kid I loved that song above all others. But interestingly I loved the ending the best. At that time, nothing in my life could move me to tears except the end of that song. At the end, Billy realizes that he and his Julie will in fact give birth to a girl. He's *sure* of it! And he sings of how fathering a girl is far different than fathering a boy. So upon hearing of the pregnancy, I *knew.*

Wendy agreed to marry me in August of 1988 citing her belief that I would be an excellent father and a decent provider. We scheduled a wedding for late October as that would give my family enough time to come to Cincinnati for the wedding. Wendy's family already lived in Cincinnati. There have been many times in my life where my act, my belief in being a man and acting like one, has been easy. That fall was one. I did exhibit some of my notorious stubbornness. I was lazy about helping to plan the wedding and other tasks Wendy asked me to carry out. But in looking at the wedding pictures, I see a scared guy, but a seemingly happy one.

Financial reality also set in upon returning from Nashville. I needed more and better work. I began work for a small musical business that specialized in flutes, The Cincinnati Fluteworks. I was a clerk. The Fluteworks offered better hourly wages than the convenience store and no midnight shifts! I walked home each day to cook Wendy a healthy lunch and returned at dinnertime to cook again. Later in the pregnancy she suffered from preeclampsia, a pregnancy related diabetes-like condition which caused her to gain huge amounts of water-weight. By February 1989 she was over 220 pounds with swollen feet and arms and was quite uncomfortable. Luckily she was a student and covered by the mandatory student health insurance. The doctors finally lost patience with the pregnancy after she was two weeks late for delivery and admitted her to the hospital for labor inducement. That painful process continued for over 30 hours before they finally decided that a 2 cm dilation was not enough and they would perform a cesarean. Our beautiful Betty was born at noon on March 3, 1989.

That first year of marriage was very stressful. It is normally so for most newlyweds. Wendy brought her own expectations to the relationship. Her idea of a husband was someone who got things done. As a homeowner she had learned many repair and renovation skills. In my past I'd only painted interiors. Carpentry, plastering, plumbing, and roof patching skills were not already extant in my skill set. But with her being pregnant then nursing the baby, those jobs fell to me, and I fell short. Wendy was constantly aggravated with me for not beginning tasks, then more aggravated when I'd begin but stop before they were done. I did manage to repair the box gutters on her 1925 row house as well as paint the entire metal roof with new silver paint.

To many readers, I'm sure the description of my behavior sounds like many men they've known. I was, after all, raised as one. The old saying, 'if it walks like a duck, and quacks like a duck…it's a duck', comes to mind. It certainly seems logical that someone who acts like a man is one. But then, could not a biological woman act this same way? It's possible. The whole notion of gender identity disorder arising from biological and/or environmental factors is a thorny patch to which we'll turn later.

I felt inadequate for many reasons; low sex drive, desire to cross-dress, low income. To add to the list failure as a handyman one day drove me right over the edge. After listening to her badger me for nearly an hour I lost my composure and began to cry. Wendy is a very strong and determined person. When she feels she has an advantage or is in the right she will press on to be certain of a complete 'victory'. She easily beat me. I cried like the day I'd proposed but in frustration. I still had dreams of winning an orchestral job. I practiced daily, often in 3 or 4 separate sessions. Wendy also dreamed of playing the horn for a living. Her dreams were as valid and important as mine, yet she had the primary baby responsibilities. In her mind, I was being unduly selfish to not put in adequate time on the house. After my breakdown, which lasted about an hour, she agreed to stop pressing me quite so vociferously and I agreed to be more diligent. It was a classic newlywed argument, except the roles were reversed. She did the yelling and I did the crying. But it worked. I got off my butt and began to take more responsibility.

We managed, we juggled, we slept less, and we worked hard. She worked hard in school and I worked hard at jobs, tasks, and practicing. I continued to audition. Auditions are expensive as one has to pay one's own way in order to have that chance at a job. I took any audition available; nearly a dozen in that year, which put a drain on our already strained finances.

One day my teacher called to say a professional brass quintet was looking for a new horn player. He'd offered my name. Thrilled was not the word, *ecstatic* was more like it. I knew I'd take the work if offered, but I never stopped to think of the effect on Wendy and our daughter. I would be out on the road for weeks at a time playing concerts all over the country. Wendy made it plain that she did not want me leaving her alone. I made it plain that this was a sacrifice I needed her to make for me. She agreed though it was obvious I was ramming the situation down her throat. It was only one of our many arguments over career.

I was able to keep my Fluteworks job by enlisting a friend to do my work there while I was away, and then allow me to do the flute work when the group was not traveling. I was only on the road about 12 weeks (off and on) during that whole year, but they were a huge strain on Wendy as she had to drive up to her mother's every morning to drop off the baby before going to school.

While it was fun and educational work for me it was no kind of life, and I soon tired of all the traveling, bad food, and smelly motel rooms. I also began to suffer with guilt for leaving Wendy with all the homework while I was gone. In the summer of 1990 I resigned from the Chicago Chamber Brass.

In July of that summer my parents had arranged a family reunion in California. However, my father's failing health was quickly taking center stage. His twenty-year battle with heart disease was nearing its inevitable end and he was hospitalized in late June with congestive heart failure. If he could be stabilized he would be put on the heart transplant waiting list. However, he did not improve. Dad had grown increasingly tired of 'being a burden' (his phraseology) to my mother. He did not have the will to fight through his illness any longer.

My mother insisted the reunion proceed and we all arrived in late July determined to enjoy ourselves in spite of his impending death. We visited dad in Redwood City, where he was hospitalized. For up to five minutes at a time he would be his old self, the happy, positive salesman. Then the strain and pain of dying would overcome his desire to appear young and healthy and he would sink into a semi-conscious resting state. We kept our visits short. The reunion was everything I expected; fun and stressful at the same time. Wendy has often commented over the years that I became a different person when around my family. I'm sure she was right, though I had no conscious knowledge of changing myself. I know now that I must have put on my 'Stewart is the person you've always thought he was' face for them. I could no longer do that all the time, but around my birth family I think I knew no other way of being.

Years later I informed each of my family members of my impending changes and why. They each commented that I'd always had a kind of underlying sadness. My mother attributed it to being a moody teenager, then a hen-pecked husband. My sister blamed my parents. She blamed them in regards to her problems and felt they must be to blame for mine too. My brother thought I was sad over my lack of career success.

It was also interesting that each one filtered their sense of my sadness through their own experience. Mom never much liked Wendy and I knew it. My sister had so much trouble with my parents, she may have felt more justified in her attitudes toward them over the years. And my brother is one of the most successful accountants I've ever heard of, becoming a full partner at Price Waterhouse in his early 30's and working out of a Manhattan office.

When my father passed on August 12, 1990 I took the next flight out to be with my mother in her time of need. Just the immediate family was there. All the spouses remained at home. We cremated his remains and followed with a memorial service. Dozens of dad's former colleagues at Prudential showed up to remember a man they all agreed taught them a great deal about not only selling insurance but about being happy people. He'd faced crushing criticism as a young boy including being told he was stupid so many times he thought it was his middle name. In the course of his career he rose to be the 81st best agent in 1971. He spent the remainder of his career helping others become better sales people. His work led him to become an outstanding motivational speaker at company conventions and an author of a number of trade journal articles.

I did not know what I felt at his passing. The death was not unexpected. He'd had his first heart attack 2 days before Christmas in 1973. From that day forward we all felt any time with him was borrowed and a blessing. I'd kind of expected his death for years and always been quite happy it had not come. His vision of me was an extremely strong motivator in my life. I not only admired and respected my father, I loved him. Pleasing him was an integral part of my psyche from my first memories until he died. Today, in my newfound personal comfort, I occasionally think of the day my sister and I traded clothes when I was five. I can still see the scowl on his face and feel the burning embarrassment at having disappointed him. I let him down on only a very few other occasions (that I know of) and each was very hard to live with.

In looking back I can see a nearly straight line of getting myself deeper and deeper into being a man, all in the hopes and expectation that I would free myself of my desires. Perhaps one difference between early transitioners and me is that for 40 years I wanted to please people. Some people are like that; *people pleasers*. I was one. I wanted everyone to like me, beginning with my parents. With dad gone I no longer had that anchor, that rock, tying me to manhood. In August of 1990 I had absolutely no idea how adrift I really was.

During that fall of 1990 there were two auditions I was eager to take, both for principal horn positions: Grand Rapids Michigan and Toledo Ohio. I prepared and took the Grand Rapids audition in September earning the usual result: 'thank you' from the committee as I was dismissed. My problem with auditions was always that they are so different from the actual work. In an orchestra you not only play your part, but you adjust your sounds to match those around you. Intonation, blend, balance, volume; they all have an effect on the total product. In an audition, however, it's just the player alone. The committee is screened so they only hear your work and are not distracted by your sex, color, height, weight, or relative beauty or ugliness. It's actually a very fair way of choosing a musician. It's just not any fun. The skill of auditioning can only truly be practiced during an actual audition. Mock auditions can help, but only the real thing has the pressure necessary in order to gain the valuable experience needed for winning. Grand Rapids quickly became yet another practice session.

Then fortune entered into my life. Lowell, my mentor, held the principal horn position in Toledo where they would be auditioning for co-principal horn that November. Until then they were in need of extra players to cover for the person who'd left. Lowell asked me to play in Toledo for one week in October of 1990.

Lowell was famous for playing horns made by Alexander, a German brand. I'd bought an Alex from him in 1987 and since meeting Lowell in 1985 had emulated his sound and style in nearly everything I played. I knew that we would sound great together, and we did. He even allowed me to play one work by myself. I played the first part on the Debussy *Premier Rhapsody* for Clarinet and Orchestra. For the other works I functioned as his assistant, playing loud or section parts to allow his lips to remain rested and flexible enough for the softer, delicate passages.

While there, I heard of an audition for the Toledo Opera, a small company which did only 2 to 3 shows per year. If I won I'd earn only about $1000, but to me it was not only another audition practice opportunity but if I did win and then won the Toledo Symphony job too, I would have even more work for myself. I took the opera audition in late October about a week after the set I'd played with the orchestra and won. It was only my second winning audition.

The Toledo Symphony audition was scheduled for November 12, three months to the day after the death of my father. Wendy and I drove up together the day before. She too would be competing to win that spot. The morning of the 12th I felt my father's presence. I don't mean as a ghost or any kind of sixth sense experience. I just felt him close in my heart and remembered how much he encouraged and supported me in my career choice. I felt I'd do well that day.

I did. The first round contained the usual 5-6 excerpts; Beethoven, Brahms, and Tchaikovsky. I knew I'd played them as well as I could; errorless, in good rhythm, and with what was to my ear good intonation. I was passed along to the second round. When all 35 players had played their first rounds the audition committee chose eight of us to play again after lunch. Wendy was not one of them and she asked to ride home with another Cincinnati player who'd also been eliminated. I ate light; just a salad. I did not want over active digestion to distract me from the nerve-wracking task ahead. We drew random numbers from a bowl. I was 6.

The second round was much more taxing and difficult, including a long excerpt from the Scherzo movement of Mahler's 5th Symphony and the long, slow, soft, and high Nocturne from Mendelssohn's *Midsummer's Night's Dream* incidental music. When I finished, I knew I'd played great. I was able to show them the vitality and intensity I feel I can bring to music and was not distracted by negative thoughts or fluttery breathing due to nerves. However, I was very, very tired at the end. I did not know how I would be able to play another round.

It's usual for a group of eight to be cut down to a smaller group of 2 or 3. I, of course, hoped to be in that group of 2 or 3, but also dreaded losing due to fatigue when I'd been doing so well.

After all eight had played, the personnel manager gathered us around to inform us of the committee's choices. However, instead of naming 2 or 3 players to play the third and possibly final round, they'd decided they'd heard a winner; me. I could hardly believe my ears. I'd done it! I'd just won a real job; one that paid something like a livable wage.

I'd been actively pursuing music since 1977. I'd practiced upwards of 10,000 hours. I'd spent well over $50,000 of my own and my parent's money to attend colleges, programs, and take auditions. Now at age 31 I was finally ready to earn a living as a horn player. I now knew what athletes felt like when they'd progressed to the championship game. But I was about to get to play the Super Bowl every day because for me, just playing at that level was a dream come true. I eagerly headed home to sweep Wendy off her feet with the news.

As I entered the house she took one look at me and said, "You won, didn't you," and slammed the bedroom door in my face.

6

Another New Life—Toledo

Wendy's anger was part jealousy and part fear. Her fear was that I, now having that coveted orchestra job, would desert her and our daughter Betty and move alone to Toledo to pursue my dreams. At this point, she knew nothing of my gender issues, nothing of my secret sessions of wearing her clothes or the internal struggles with which I'd suffered my whole life. She knew only the nearly obsessive man who seemed to put his own career and practice schedule above his family. She also knew only the 'come here-go away' guy who once he had the love of a good woman would then seemingly squander it by ignoring the very person who'd given that love. It took me a number of years to understand her fear that day. For me, it seemed a clear case of jealousy, which I still maintain was a part of the picture. I took the next few hours to assure her that I loved her and was not in any way planning a life without her or our beloved child. Wendy's final quarters of master degree work at CCM were still ahead of her. She would obviously be staying in Cincinnati, at least until the summer of 1991.

Lowell, my mentor, teacher, and now professional colleague, offered to put me up for the first six weeks or so of my tenure in Toledo. I began work there with a pops concert featuring The Canadian Brass in late November 1990. During the days (the orchestra rehearsed in the evenings to accommodate orchestra members who were also teachers or had day jobs) I would look for housing. Very soon I found I was overwhelmed with the need to dress more completely than I ever had before. I knew I was in a very precarious situation. I was a guest in another person's home. I had no right to privacy, though I thought I would be granted some as his guest. Beside myself with feminine thoughts in a new and very uncomfortable way, I headed up to the local Meijer. I thought that if I just bought what I wanted and wore it, I could get back to my life. I gritted my teeth, stared down the clerk, and walked out with a blue skirt, tan top, underwear, and, for the first time, shoes. I had to guess at sizes. I was disappointed to find that even those were too small. "What did you expect, you freak," I asked myself. "You're a man, for God's sake!"

Like so many cross dressers and transsexuals early in their struggle with this condition I was thrilled with my purchases, but soon the guilt overwhelmed me and I resolved to discard my $75 dollars worth of new clothes. This 'logic' is quite common in the gender variant community; it even has a name: purging. I was a ritual purger. I'd always thrown away any clothes that I'd bought for the silly reason that if I did not have them around I though I would not dress. Laughable failed logic! But the most disturbing thing was my overwhelming *need* to dress, which came over me like a hurricane nearly the moment I'd arrived for my new job.

The 'experts' say that a cross-dresser must dress to relieve stress. I certainly had a great deal of stress at that time. However, in my opinion, the majority of the stress was due to the gender conflict itself, not the move or job change or necessary separation from my family. My new position represented a dream come true for me. And in truth, all of my time at work was great. I loved my job from the first moment to this very day. It was, as always, time *alone* that was my enemy. When alone I was torn apart by guilt, shame, and the overwhelming desire to dress and appear as a woman. I still was not ready to think clearly enough to know whether I actually wanted to be a woman.

◆　　　◆　　　◆

My new colleagues were eager to help me find the best place to live. They suggested a number of nice areas of town. I soon found I could not afford to live in any of those 'symphony member approved' neighborhoods. Neither could I just rent any old apartment. I needed a house. Practicing is a noisy affair for a brass player. My previous encounters with apartment dwelling were that the neighbors would be quick with their complaining if I played at all. A house was a minimum. There were affordable houses for rent in Toledo, that's one of its strengths. I found a 2-bedroom bungalow for only $300 a month which was still over one-third of my take home pay! I made it my residence over New Year's weekend 1990/91.

Wendy and Betty were there to help (Betty helped by being 'terminally cute' as we used to say) and Wendy's stepfather pulled a trailer up for us. We treated him to dinner after the easy move (only 5-6 pieces of furniture) and he headed home. Wendy, Betty and I spent our first night together in our new home on January 1, 1991. But she headed back to Cincinnati the very next day.

She seemed to be cold toward me and had since my victory, as if she didn't quite believe that I was truly interested in remaining married to her. In fact, I was *dreading* her departure. I was only dimly aware of how much I needed her. I knew from her absences from our home in Cincinnati that when I was alone I would think of and often engage in dressing.

I remembered one evening a few months before. Wendy had recently won a horn position of her own—4th horn in a metropolitan orchestra near Cincinnati. One evening while she was at rehearsal and I remained home with Betty, I gave in to my needs and rifled her closet. She had a very nice green sweater dress which fit me well. I put it on, and since Betty was down for the night and I knew I had time before Wendy came home, I thought I'd try out some of her make-up.

As the time of Wendy's arrival home drew near, I took off her dress and washed my face to remove the make-up. But I'd also never worn mascara before and was not familiar with its 'difficult to remove' properties. I did a poor job.

Wendy walked in. I kissed her hello and she said, "Are you wearing mascara?!"

Oops! In all the years I'd dressed I'd never to my knowledge been caught, not even in my foolish night walk in Nashville. Now here, with no warning; *caught*.

"Oh, yeah, I was bored and saw it in the bathroom and wondered what it would look like if I put it on. I guess I didn't get it off very well." Whew! I delivered the lie like a pro. Hell, I could be a politician! I'm actually a very poor liar. But in this case the stakes were so high and my denial and repression so deep, that I could not even comprehend the consequences of failing to pull off the cover story. Everyone knows the best lies are simply variations on or portions of the truth. Hence my line, while far from the complete story, was technically correct. I was bored. Boredom and being alone had always been my enemy because that's when I thought of dressing. And I did try it and I did fail to get it all off. However my 'confident in my masculinity' stance was pure bull. Now with months of lonely living ahead, I dared not think of what lengths to which I might go to relieve my boredom.

The TSO schedule had some big holes in it and I drove down to Cincinnati at least 3-4 times a month. But with the yawning hours of the weekdays open before heading to rehearsal in the evening, my mind began to dwell on my topic constantly. I soon found the local public library and drawing myself up with as much dignity as I could, used the computerized card catalog to research the topic.

I've since read that thousands of people like me have done exactly the same thing. They've found the books and then read them there in the library to avoid the stares of the clerks. But the Toledo-Lucas County Public Library had few books on the subject of transvestism. The ones they had described men who were highly sexual, both in regards to women's clothes and with their wives. They described men who were high functioning. In other words, those guys were pretty much just guys. They worked, they were married, and their hobby was dressing in women's clothing.

I thought about my history with dressing, but the guilt and shame made introspection very difficult. At age 30 I was extremely tired of the fight and despaired of ever being free of the desire to dress. Being willing to even read relevant books was a huge step forward. I was at the library as often as I could be. The books were dry sociological tomes that dealt with the topic in as scientific way as possible. While I found them interesting, I needed to see some pictures. I knew that I looked horrible whenever I dressed and wondered what magical transformations others were capable. I also looked for the Christine Jorgensen story. I'd heard of the book as a child but in dozens of secret card catalog searches had never even found a library that stocked one, as if the mere presence of that book would somehow contaminate the others.

Now, fully transitioned, I'm a good friend with a library professional. She informs me that those kinds of 'too embarrassed to check out' books were theft bait for years. Poor slobs desperate for information but too ashamed to even sit in the library and read the book would, in their desperation, find a way to smuggle those kinds of books out of the building. Libraries all over the country simply gave up and either did not replace many of the most attractive books or put them in the stacks, which would require a written request from a patron in order to check them out. In Toledo that in the stack technique sure worked with me. I never asked them for anything.

One book they did have out for the public was the Renee Richards autobiography, *Second Serve*. After standing in the aisles and reading it for an hour I decided I was being silly. I realized I was afraid of what some anonymous library employee would think of me. "Why should I care," I thought. "I'm breaking no laws. The book is in the library, for God's sake! It's there to be checked out." So down I went to the front desk and checked out the book. I thought of those war-based aphorisms like 'the best defense is a good offense' and decided that by being willing to look the clerk in the eye and have my body language say 'you wanna make something of me for checking out this book? Go right ahead and stare, I don't give a shit'. It was a similar stance to another trait I learned years before; walking.

When I was young and living in neighborhoods that were dangerous for me, I found that by walking in a certain way I could repel others and reach my goal of being left alone. It was a kind of determined stomp, which would include eye contact with any males who would approach followed by a quick but friendly 'how ya' doin'' kind of nod. This worked especially well in ethnic neighborhoods. I found I could walk in largely black and Hispanic areas without being hassled. The older I got the more ingrained this style of walking became. In fact, it was one of my first tasks when deciding to transition; learn to walk in a more feminine way. But since the masculine technique was just so much veneer in the first place, it was not a terribly difficult task to strip it away and reveal a more natural walk.

My book checkout fears were, of course, unfounded. The library professionals have seen all kinds of books cross their desks and if they spent their days looking at customers cross-eyed they'd not only soon get tired eyes, but also probably engender complaints from the customers for judgementalism.

I got home, made some coffee, and sat down to read the Richards. I finished in four uninterrupted hours. Though I'd never applied the label 'transsexual' to myself, the story of Dr. Richard Raskind resonated with me. I felt I was having a heart to heart talk with someone who'd suffered much of the same life anguish I had over the years. But I also did not want the label Dr. Richards finally so easily embraced. I was prepared to admit to being a transvestite. A cross dresser, as they prefer to be called, was someone who could find a balance between a life long compulsion and wife, children, and job.

No words could describe those first five months of 1991. When not reading, I was wrapped up in work. I struggled to impress my colleagues with my ability at work while figuratively tearing myself apart while at home. Though I was holding a principal horn position, I had very little experience.

The conundrum of orchestral playing is that while it is often a difficult task, it will never 'work out' all aspects of the player's technique equally. Great players were those who daily exercised the difficult areas of technique and strived to improve the weaker ones. It's a bit like the relationship between athletics and weight lifting. Today, nearly all athletes, including many golfers, lift weights. They do that because they've found that the balanced strength one can achieve makes possible a more relaxed and efficient use of the body in their sport. All performing musicians are athletes, albeit artistic ones.

My solitary existence made my historical pattern of never being alone nearly impossible to maintain. For the first time in my life, I found I had to deal with daily, often constant, thoughts of myself as a woman. I'd never before been bothered by my feminine thoughts while practicing or performing. Now, they never left me. At that time, I did not make any connection between my father's death and the onslaught of disturbing thoughts. Though I hated the fact that I could not shut off the flow of thoughts as I had always done in the past, I also began to weaken in my resolve to kill it once and for all.

In my twenties I matured enough to know that just dressing and masturbating would not forever banish the thoughts. In that decade I found that no matter what I did the thoughts would eventually come back. Now, in my early thirties, my mind raised the stakes; as if to say, 'Hey! Did you forget me? I'm still here and I'm damn tired of you ignoring me!' So with the newly found bravado and 'I don't care what you think' attitude I'd used at Meijer and the library, I went to the local used clothing store to look around. I could not even be honest about the fact that I knew I was going there to buy all the clothes that I wanted but had never allowed myself to have. Money being tight, I got to 'enjoy' the added taint of guilt over spending money we could not really afford to spend. But I needed to know! I needed to dress and see what I would look like.

I found what I wanted. I stared down the clerk, who was far less professional than the ones at the library and openly smirked at my choices. I had not tried anything on. I did not yet have a death wish! So my choices of size were mere guesses based on holding up the blouses, skirts, and pants to my eye. I'd not even thought enough ahead to bring a tape measure. I did buy my first bra, though I drew the line at used underwear. If I could stand the stares of the used clothes store clerk, what difference would there be with the clerk at Kmart?

For a few days, I reveled in being able to dress as I chose any time I was home. I cooked, cleaned, practiced, and watched television or read books. But soon I noticed that I could not do most of the normal things the rest of the world can do. I could not go for a walk, or go grocery shopping, or walk the dog, or go to a movie. I was stuck in my little bubble.

"Well," I thought, "I can at least go let the dog out into the yard late in the evening, when it's dark. If anyone saw me, they might just think it was my wife." So I stepped out my front door dressed fully in feminine clothes for the first time in the late winter of 1991.

"But my hair is so short," I lamented. Even standing in the darkened yard, I knew that anyone looking would be able to see that it was me, their male horn playing neighbor standing there in a dress.

I headed to the local wig store. Taking purchases up to an anonymous clerk at a large retail store is one thing. Shopping for a wig involves a one on one relationship with a sales-professional. Even the local budget wig shop was run the same way. I decided to use the costume party excuse. I'm positive she saw right through me but played along for my benefit. I quickly realized that shop owners just want your money. They may choose to feel superior when a male-bodied person wants to buy women's things, but they'll mostly hide that if they can in order to get your money. In that way small shops, though more personal, can often be more accepting. Some cross dressers even call ahead to establish that the shop owner would be ok with them shopping there. Business people will often offer to work with men after hours to make their experience more pleasant. With private appointments comes freedom to try on the clothes as well.

I, however, was not yet accepting of myself. I was simply driven. So I lied and got what I wanted. I went right home, dressed, and went to my mirror to put the wig on for the first time. I'd not tried it on in the store. I needed to stay with my cover story in order to keep my composure, so thought I should adopt an 'I don't really care how it looks' position. But when I slipped the wig over my 2-inch hair I was absolutely thrilled. I think my experience that winter and spring is the essence of the gender confusion stage of gender dysphoria. The dysphoric sufferer is both attracted to and repelled by their gender issues. In my case, while I hated that aspect of myself, it felt so good to see in the mirror a vision I'd dreamed of my entire life.

I think the mind quickly tires of self hate. It is a draining existence. Some transgendered people cannot find a way to avoid their dilemma and they suffer greatly. Others, like me, twist their minds in knots to compartmentalize the confusion in order to exist in the world. But eventually we all begin to show the wear the strain has caused. In the case of someone not able to deny their feelings they either learn to accept that part of themselves (and in all likelihood transition) or they commit suicide. In cases like mine where the sufferer's ability to lie to him or herself is draining away, the same process begins to take place though more slowly. I'd never, to that point, been suicidal over the issue and though I later learned that I was beginning a long decade of mild depression around this time, I was somewhat content to begin to integrate dressing with the rest of my life.

Whenever I thought of telling Wendy a cold fear washed over me, and I knew that I had to continue to keep this a secret. Wendy's trips to Toledo around that time entailed me carefully packaging my things and finding the best hiding place I could.

My struggle also had an effect on my work. While I generally impressed my new colleagues, there were days when I found it quite difficult to concentrate. Missed notes and poor intonation were the usual offenses. The missed notes were obvious, but intonation is a far more elusive quality in the first place. I've listened to recordings from this period and I generally sound quite good; better than a couple of years later in fact when I was struggling to improve my intonation. But new players will often rise to the challenge of earning tenure only to fall back a bit in their playing once they've received it. In my case, earning that coveted tenure was very, very important. In April of 1991 the orchestra had scheduled Frank Martin's *Concerto for Seven Winds and Orchestra*. Lowell was out of town that week playing somewhere else in the world, so it fell to me to play the horn part in that soloistic work. Like all the pieces we performed, I did my homework delivering two excellent performances. My colleagues were impressed. In the first six months in Toledo, I played principal on Dvorak 7th Symphony, Bruckner's 6th Symphony, Brahms Symphony No. 2, Respighi's *Roman Festivals* and the Rachmaninoff Piano Concerto No. 2.

As I grew more comfortable with my newfound awareness of myself, of my need to express a more feminine nature, I sought to find others like myself. I knew that there might just be a bar in town that either allowed cross-dressers, or actually offered shows, like the famous *Finnocihio's* in San Francisco. I decided I'd let my fingers do the walking and called bars right out of the phone book.

"Hi, could you tell me which bar caters to the dressers?"

"The hell you say!"

"You know, men who dress like women."

"Damn Fuckin' Fags."

I got through to about a half dozen till I reached a nice boy who said, "Oh, honey, you want to go to *Caesar's* on Erie. Open Friday, Saturday, and Sunday. They've got great live shows; just what you're looking for. Have fun!"

On a Friday night in March 1991, I decided to go to *Caesar's*. I dressed as Stewart for I still felt I must look horrible. It was a reconnaissance mission of sorts. I was interested in seeing exactly how good or bad the majority of the people looked; people meaning men dressed like women.

My first time there I sat alone. I wasn't there to find a date, make small talk, or 'cruise'. I was there to observe, to learn. The show began as I enjoyed a Budweiser. "Wow," "Holy Shit," and other expletive-laden compliments flooded my mind. These women (for they looked like nothing but) were beautiful. After the 45-minute show they turned up the lights and the radio while the girls took a break. A couple of them came out to talk with friends and I wandered over in order to get a better look. Then I noticed the thick pancake make-up to cover the beard and their large masculine features like their hands and foreheads.

I was there to learn and I did. I learned that, up close, these professionals did not look like women to me. I wondered if it was the foreknowledge that I had, knowing they were men, which allowed me to see the male in them. I realized I wanted them to look perfect. I wanted to know it was *possible* to lead a dual life. I could not imagine giving up my job. It was a dream of mine to play the French horn at the professional level, and I could not let it go so soon. But I could also not let go of the thoughts I had flooding my mind. They were like the water behind a dam. I'd dammed up the thoughts, visions, and desires for my entire life. There was quite a bit of material behind that dam. For some reason I did not then know, that dam broke and I was being flooded. I struggled daily to get my work done, my responsibilities carried out, and to retain my sense of rightness in the world. Each day I seemed to lose myself to the struggle.

While at *Caesar's* I found a newsletter type publication. Inside was a phone number for *Crossroads*, a cross-dresser's support group based in Michigan. I called and reached Tanya. Tanya sounded like Terrell, but I'd known what to expect. I made an appointment with Tanya to meet and discuss their club/support group.

Because some people might be offended by the group and actually be willing to hurt the members, they screened each potential new member to be sure they were honest and sincere. We met at a White Castle in suburban Detroit. She was a middle aged Asian businessman. We ordered coffee and grabbed the rear booth for privacy. She showed me the photo albums from meetings and parties. Some people made quite ugly women and some were better looking than your average woman. Tanya showed me a picture of her as Tanya.

"Wow," I offered, honestly reacting to how much better she looked as Tanya than she did as a balding corporate drone. She offered that she thought I would make a lovely girl and they'd enjoy having me come to the next meeting.

Tanya said, "Dressing is highly encouraged, but optional."

"Oh no, I'll dress," I said.

On the appointed day some week or so later I packed with great care: wig, clothes, make-up (which I'd recently bought at the drug store with *no* idea of what I needed, let alone *should* be buying), and my purse (a girl's not ready to leave the house without her purse!). The meeting was scheduled for 6pm at a hotel near Detroit Metro Airport with the dressing room opening at 5:30 for those who could not come dressed, like me.

I was alone in the dressing room so did not have to have anyone else see my poor make-up application skills. I made my way to the meeting. It was the first time I'd ever let a soul see me dressed as a girl. I thought I'd be more nervous but I actually felt very comfortable. Soon people came by to introduce themselves. I met a contractor, a truck driver, and a police officer. There was also another police officer, but not dressed. He was trying to please his wife by not dressing, so he just came to see friends. It was mostly business people. I was the only artistic type there. I heard a room full of male voices. The few female voices were the three wives present. In comparison to the rest of us, these women looked like goddesses. Shortly after my transition to full time some ten years later I would often joke that God put transsexuals on the earth to make usual women (as opposed to us; *unusual* women) feel more beautiful.

These wonderful women were so supportive of their husbands they would accompany them to faceless hotel meeting rooms so their men could dress like women. While there, I heard no dates being arranged, and I saw no touching except between some married couples. In fact the meeting was quite boring with minutes being read, plans being made for upcoming summer parties, and an upcoming election for board members. Then they mentioned 'The Be-All'

'The what-all,' I wondered. A national organization hosted an event in the Midwest each June called the 'Be All You Want To Be' event. It reminded me of an army advertising slogan common at that time. Many Crossroads members were planning on going to the 'Be-All', as they called it. The host city was Cleveland in June 1991.

"Wow," I thought, "A whole weekend as Sandra with lots of other people like me. I won't get laughed at much, if at all, and I can see whether my dreams really make any sense or not." I decided then and there that I would go.

But before that June weekend there were eight weeks of symphony season left to perform. Still ahead I had the aforementioned Martin concerto, Respighi *Roman Festivals*, and the Rachmaninoff Second Concerto. With the finding of Crossroads and learning of the 'Be-All', I relaxed a bit and felt a lessening of the intense dysphoria, or gender discomfort, which had so plagued me since winning the Toledo position.

But as those weeks progressed, the flooding of my psyche with cross-gendered feelings began to intensify yet again. I found I needed to go out; to be in the world as Sandra. At first, I just walked around my block late on a dark evening. I was a walking billboard figuratively screaming for people to look at me, though that was not my conscious intention. I wore a skirt, top, shoes, wig, and make-up while out for a walk at 11:30pm. This was actually more dangerous than my evening walk in Nashville. Though I'd never really noticed, women don't go walking the neighborhood after dark, especially dressed in what could be described as Sunday church clothes or office wear. Instead of blending in, I was drawing attention to myself by breaking rules every natural born woman knows by the time she's an adult.

After my walk around the block, I found it very easy to hop in my car and head out. I went to *Caesar's* even though I found it an irritating place to be due to the loud music and sexually charged atmosphere. My idea of a nice bar is one where the music is soft and conversation can actually take place. While at *Cae-*

sar's, I spoke to another transgendered person who mentioned the *Scenic Bar*, a lesbian place around the corner where cross-dressers were allowed to enter, though no men were allowed. Looking for relief from the noise, I headed out on foot and was admitted. I got a booth and decided women probably didn't drink Budweiser from a bottle, so I ordered a daiquiri. It was silly behavior really. Women drink what they like and they dress any way they want. In the *Scenic Bar* the women were all in jeans and short-sleeved shirts or tanks with sneakers. I wore a dress. I must have looked ridiculous. In my time in lesbian bars most of the women I've seen were quite short, under 5'5". I, at 6'2", literally stood out. On my third or fourth trip there a woman came over to talk.

Sliding into the booth with me she said, "How do you like *Scenic?*"

"It's...good," I said. Ever the doofus.

"So, do you like men or women?"

"Both," I replied, replying honestly before I could censor myself.

"Well, you should check out Atlanta. There are huge numbers of people like you there. So many guys, it would make your head spin. You'd do well there." Obviously, she only heard the men part. I've come to realize that most gay people are firmly convinced that cross-dressers, and especially transsexuals, are just gay folks who have a hard time admitting their own homosexuality.

After a May Crossroads meeting, another member and her transsexual girlfriend invited me to their home on the upcoming Saturday night for some socializing. I knew I first had a concert to play, one with a live radio broadcast to boot, but agreed to head up there as soon as I was done. That Saturday I packed my clothes and accessories headed to the concert. On the program that night was the *Roman Festivals* and the Rachmaninoff Second Concerto with Andre Watts as soloist. He would also be performing the Tchaikovsky First Concerto, but that work on the second half, and I was not scheduled to play the Tchaikovsky.

I felt the *Roman Festivals* went great though later heard the tape and was appalled by my intonation at one critical place. In the Rachmaninoff, I *knew* I had trouble. There is a wonderful moment in the first movement when the piece seems to slow to a complete stop, only to be resurrected by the beautiful second theme played alone by the solo horn. I loved that moment and had since I was a child. I wanted to play that spot very well. That night I became aware of a pattern, which I still struggle with today: the more I love a work or a passage, the harder it is for me to perform it well. It's as if my memory of so many perfect performances on recordings clouds my vision and sets the bar just out of reach. The problem was with my air, which got tighter the more I worried about the passage. When one gets nervous breathing becomes shallow. With string players or percussionists, this shortening of the breath is not an inherently disruptive problem. With a wind player it can be devastating. I struggled through that beautiful spot taking extra breaths because my racing heart used up what air I'd taken far too soon. The sound was tight, ugly, and out of tune. But I did not miss any notes. I've come to label that kind of playing as 'survival mode'. I made no music in that spot, no art was re-created, only employment survival.

Good or bad, we must get up from our chairs and leave the stage. I may have been a big believer in the 'act as if' principle when I was younger, but I still struggled to treat winning and losing the same as an adult and professional musician. I stormed off the stage both angry and eager. When I made it to my car, I could tell I was smiling. Not because I'd failed that night, for I had not, I'd only not succeeded, but because I was off to Detroit to enjoy an entire evening as Sandra. I had no work the next day and no plans to go to Cincinnati.

I arrived in the suburbs of Detroit about 90 minutes later. I dressed and they agreed to give me some make up lessons. I was so thrilled I paid little attention to what they said. When they were done I looked better than I ever thought I could, but it still looked like me in mirror. I was disappointed. I'd been hoping for some huge transformative experience. Instead I looked like Stewart with a great shave and a decent make-up job in some rather frumpy clothes.

"Oh well," I thought. "I'm here, I feel good, and I might as well have a good time."

We talked, we walked around the house a few times, and the time passed as if it were on amphetamines. All too soon it was 4:30am and I realized I'd probably outstayed my welcome. Though they invited me to take their couch I opted to leave.

"You can change upstairs where you did when you came in," my hostess said.

"Actually, I'd prefer to drive home this way," I answered.

"You know, that can be dangerous. What if you get stopped by the police or the car breaks down? Men dressed as women are not usually treated very well by anyone you know."

I knew that, but I also knew that taking off my clothes was the last thing in the world I wanted to do. I felt free and light in a way I'd never known. I was not feeling sexual and had not for hours. While I still got a good feeling from wearing the clothes, I always looked forward to the passing of the sexually charged atmosphere that always seemed to accompany dressing. I simply felt good in a way I could not describe. I could not allow myself to end the experience.

I think that after 25 active years of hiding my feelings, learning a way of being that was acceptable to my family and circle of acquaintances, and actively putting down my feminine feelings, I was like a prisoner released from solitary confinement. The sun and the air felt so good I did not care if it was my last day on earth. I wanted those good feelings to remain. So I got in my car and headed south.

As I took my exit off the freeway I knew I was still too *up* to go home and go to bed, so I headed down to *Caesar's*. They had an all night coffee shop next door which picked up where the bar left off at 2am. It was 6am and I decided I'd get breakfast.

While I ate my pancakes, a young man came over. "Hey, you feel like having some company?"

"Oh, um, no. I'm, um, married actually," I answered.

"Sure honey, I know, and it's ok! I'd *love* to spend some time with you." The cook/waiter/owner just ignored us. I guess he'd seen and heard it all a million times.

"No really, I'm married; happily so. This is, like, my hobby. I'm not here to pick up a date, though you look very nice," I added.

"Well, I think you're a real lady. I'd love to be with you. Only $50; special just for you."

Oh shit, a professional. I smirked at that.

"No, I'm sorry. I won't do that to my wife." I ended up giving him a ride since he was going in the same direction I was. He kept up the sales pitch all the way, firmly convinced as many gay people seem to be, that any man in women's clothing is engaged in a form of sexual acting out.

I finally got home about 7am on that Sunday morning in May. I still did not want to take my clothes off. In part I was afraid I'd want to masturbate and did not want to ruin my whole vision of being a woman by exposing and touching my own penis. The other part was I felt so *right*; the thought of leaving the house as Stewart again was not appealing. Also, in my fatigue, I began to think of all the people I'd deceived over the years. I thought of my family, my friends, and now my own wife. How long was I willing for this to remain my secret? I was sick from keeping it secret and part of my severe dysphoria with gender over the last six months was due to it being a secret.

I'd always enjoyed a great relationship with my sister. We'd talked over the years, mostly about her troubles and her struggle with overcoming her early years. I felt I could tell her and she'd understand, so I picked up the phone.

"Yeah, what do you want," she croaked in her sleepy gauzy voice. She'd been a smoker since age 12 and had that characteristic gravel in her voice.

"Hi, it's…Stewart."

"Stewart! Gosh, it's early. Is something wrong?"

"No, but I have something I need to tell you. Are you sitting down? Are you ok to hear something?"

"Stewart, you don't sound good. What's wrong? Just tell me what's wrong."

"I'm…I'm sitting here…in a dress. And wig, make-up, and jewelry. I just got back from being out all night dressed this way. I had a *great* time. I've done this since I was little and…well, I just needed to tell someone."

"*God*…well—do you…like, do you want to have a sex change?"

"Oh no! Of course I don't. I love being a guy. I just need to dress like a girl sometimes." And that was where my honesty stopped and the bullshit ran free once again. When I had to face all of this again less than ten years later, this scene replayed over and over in my mind. When I told my sister how I felt and the first question out of her mouth was about the very thing I knew I'd been thinking all evening, I just could not face that truth. I told a lie I could accept in order to get through that moment.

"No," I'd said, "I enjoy being a man". The truth was I was struggling to be one and though I enjoyed what men could *have,* position, power, money, and status (who wouldn't!), I'd found being a man an enormous burden my whole life.

We talked for over an hour. I told her of my overwhelming feelings since I'd moved to Toledo. She related my recent trouble to dad's death in an intuitive leap I'd not to that point made. I covered my history with the situation and my plans for the future. She asked about my family and how this would affect them. Not at all, I said. I'd heard from others in Crossroads about wives who could not handle a husband's cross-dressing. The divorce usually left him with no visitation and lots of alimony to pay. Though I was chafing at my role as husband and father it was a role I wanted. That is the essence of gender dysphoria. It's confusion about one's gender *role.* I wanted to be both the man I'd worked so hard to be; the husband, father, musician, and citizen, and a woman. In my heart, which is only fully accessible in the past tense, I knew that I was not much like my cross-dressing acquaintances in Crossroads, I was much more like the transsexuals I'd read about, wanting to be a girl and not just look somewhat like one for a few hours. But in my confusion I thought I could walk a line between the two.

7

Mental Illness

Over the years that I dealt with my desire to cross-dress and allow feminine feelings I never felt myself to be mentally ill, though by definition in the Diagnostic and Statistical Manual, the book by which psychiatrists and psychologists determine how best to help people presenting for treatment, I was. Whether I was called a fetishistic cross-dresser or a sufferer from Gender Identity Disorder (GID) was totally dependent on my level of honesty. This entire recounting of my life is, by the very nature of retrospection, subject to the trap of rewriting history. I've done my best to keep spin out of the story and only tell the events as I truly remember them. As for my thoughts and feelings, since I was so closed off and secretive even from myself, those are far harder to obtain. But even in my specially built closet, I had thoughts about this topic and have disclosed those where applicable in the story, from the complete confusion of my primary school years, to the knowledge of the relief found in teenage cross-dressing (although believing that after each episode I would never do it again), to my realization in my 20's that it was a part of me although one I hated. By the time I reached my thirties, marriage, the death of my father, and my newfound musical success, the stress of denying the unwanted parts and maintaining my carefully crafted persona started to show in my inability to cover the condition. Hence, my increased dressing and travel in public en femme. Through the latter I found some scant relief.

By increasing my acceptance of the condition I improved my life, but by choosing to continue hiding the truth from my spouse I in fact made my life even more stressful. Up to then my hiding was largely from myself, and that allowed me to exist and move in the world as Stewart in a fairly un-conflicted way. I coped by choosing to think about only what I chose to think about; to compartmentalize my mind even more and stay on task nearly all the time. At work I focused on my horn playing, on the music, and tasks at hand. At home alone I was wide open to how I really felt and what I truly needed.

The approaching 'Be-All' excited me greatly, though not in a sexual way. This is often the most difficult part for people not familiar with the transsexual phenomena to believe, that a part of one's very *identity* could be in doubt. That doubt is, in essence, the crux of Gender Identity Disorder (GID).

Between the end of the symphony season in May of 1991 and the 'Be-All' in June I went out a few times in female attire. Most of my trips were to the Scenic Bar, Caesar's, or Blu Jeans. But one night after being at Scenic I got a wild idea, I just had to go out where 'regular' people were and see how well I passed. It was stupid really because I knew in my heart that I was a wreck. I could see it in the mirror but the honesty to acknowledge it just made me feel bad, so I pretended my wish to look good would suffice.

I drove out to a suburban grocery store. It was about half past midnight. I was wearing a dress, pumps and a wig, not anyone's typical attire for a midnight run to the grocery! I felt a tingle of thrill as I headed to the lights of the store. It reminded me of the kind of excitement one gets when about to step into the limelight. I headed for the cosmetics aisle. My makeup skills were terrible so I thought I could find some better products.

I'd not taken ten steps when I heard, in a loud male voice, "Oh my God! It's a man!" We've all seen cartoons where someone becomes embarrassed and physically shrinks. After hearing the comment I knew exactly what that felt like. I strode on confidently though and made my selections.

As I approached the clerk, she had the 'deer in the headlights' look on her face that I've seen a few other times. "Nice night," I offered.

"Uh huh," she groaned.

◆   ◆   ◆

In the previous six weeks I'd traveled to Detroit to shop at a cross-dresser's specialty shop called Lavender and Lace, and spent nearly $800 in clothes, shoes, wigs, and make-up. Now with the 'Be-All' I was spending another $300 in hotel and conference fees. Ignoring my guilt about the money I packed my bags and headed for Cleveland. Once there, I eagerly showered, shaved, and dressed. The first event was dinner in the dining room followed by most of the girls heading to the bar to drink and talk.

After an hour or so in the bar, a man came over to our table to ask a question. "Excuse me, but somebody told me that all of you here a really men. Is that true?"

"Yes," we all chimed in. Then one girl began the tedious explanation of male cross-dressing and how we're not perverted, pedophilic, deviant, or harmful. He seemed amazed that men could look so good, though I was sure at the time he was just secretly intrigued by us, perhaps even harboring a desire to join us. As I looked around the table my newfound acquaintances all looked like men in drag to me, so even though I felt great I was sure I looked no better (and probably worse) than them. It's hard to believe a 6'2" person with poorly covered beard shadow is a woman. My unacknowledged thoughts were: 'why be just a cross-dresser when one could go further, get beard removal, take hormones, and live full time?'

But my skill at compartmentalizing thoughts allowed me to shove that idea down and close the lid. Thoughts like that, I knew, would lead to other thoughts like: 'What about my marriage and my daughter? What about my job? They'd never let a transsexual keep that wonderful job! What about my mother and siblings? They would surely reject me if they knew. Do I really want to lose everything and be completely cut off and alone? I've worked very hard to get what I have; job, family, and the respect of others. Is that not worth keeping?'

Those were the fears, the root causes of continued hiding. One might wonder, 'then why not then simply maintain a complete rejection of any feminine expression? Would that not best insure that I could keep all the things I feared losing if my problem came to light?' But I could not. I know no better way to say it but that I could no longer keep up the near 100% facade of Stewart. I needed some relief; some respite from my created character.

The defining moment of the weekend in Cleveland came on the second night, Saturday evening, at the banquet that was the centerpiece of the convention. Some months before, just after my move to Toledo, I called the International Foundation for Gender Expression, IFGE, located in Boston. On the phone I spoke with a woman, a transwoman, who helped direct me to greater acceptance of myself and gave me suggestions on how to proceed.

At the door to the dinner I could see by her nametag that before me was the very woman who had helped. I can't imagine she remembered me, but even so after taking one look at me she said, "You look so happy! It's wonderful to see!"

The next day I decided to get a make-over from Jim Bridges, a 'make-up artist to the stars' kind of person from California. I also bought a new and better wig. After my makeover I had a photograph taken. Viewing that picture was both thrilling and disgusting. Thrilling in that I so much liked what I saw. I could see that I was happy; it radiated from my entire being in that picture. I hated it though, because I still saw me—Stewart...a man. Once again the revulsion was largely unacknowledged, though I was aware of somehow being uncomfortable with the photo. On the drive home that afternoon I took it out and looked at it over and over, thrilled and repulsed at the same time.

While on that drive home to Toledo my need to tell Wendy became a physical pain. I would imagine it's akin to the feeling a child would have after breaking a neighbor's window and then instead of knocking on their door to tell them the child instead goes home, hoping the neighbors, and the child itself, will forget. The lie, or withholding of the truth, eventually becomes far worse than truth's recitation. The next morning I sped down to Cincinnati to rejoin my family. I'd made up some story about why I needed to remain in Toledo over that weekend.

Wendy had been a horsewoman since her teenage years when a friend gave her a pony. Then, in 1991, she kept her pair of horses on her stepfather's three hundred acre wooded tract in Northern Kentucky. While heading down there to meet up with her mother and stepfather, I could hold my truth no longer.

With Betty asleep in her car seat I began. "Wendy, I need to tell you why I did not come home last weekend." I paused, unsure how to tell her my version of the truth; how to walk a line between total honesty and the compassionate withholding of important information. In a flash I could see the end of my family and my freedom to see Betty. But I was sick of the hiding. I had to tell her what I knew.

"What? Just tell me, its ok," she said.

I took a deep breath and began. "For my whole life, I've wanted to dress in women's clothes. It's just a…hobby. I love you and don't want anything to come between us, but I…I just need to do that."

"Oh, cool! You know when I was in high school, we had a costume party and I went as a lumberjack. I got a fake beard and padded one of my brother's plaid shirts with foam so I looked huge! People were shocked and really kind of disgusted. It was funny! I had a great time. You know, I've always been kind of counter culture. That really shocked them. And people thought they knew me!"

"No, Wendy, actually that's not really what I'm talking about. You're talking about some *party*. I'm talking about going to Cleveland this past weekend and spending the whole time dressed as a woman. Here, this is a picture I had taken there."

She reluctantly looked at the photo. "Oh," long silence. "Well…you certainly look happy in this picture."

I hated the telling, but had to do it. "I don't know what else to say. I needed you to know."

The enormity of the situation began to break over her. "I don't know what to say either! You blurt out that you've always wanted to dress in women's clothes. What does that mean? Do you want a divorce? Are you going to get a sex change?

What kind of example will that set for Betty? You're looking at me like you want an answer *now*. I can't do that. This is huge! I've got to think about this. Let's just get to the farm and meet up with Mom and Burt and we'll talk about this another time."

The truth was that since my job in Toledo began, we'd been having great difficulty in our marriage. Was the trouble due to the separation, the dressing, my lies, her anger at me for winning and wanting her to move? I did not know. It was all jumbled up in my mind.

◆   ◆   ◆

Wendy decided we would house sit for a colleague in Dayton for the summer so after our weekend in Kentucky, we packed again and headed to Dayton to live in a strange house. I hated it. She knew I preferred not to house sit. While there she insisted we visit a marriage counselor. It seemed to me I went from the thrill of the 'Be-All' to the horrible pit of getting looked at askance by my spouse and heading to marriage counseling in a mere moment.

Marriage counseling is neither fish nor fowl, not hot or cold, not for one partner or the other. Its sole purpose is to improve the relationship. I'm sure we visited an experienced and studied professional.

But twenty minutes into 'So, tell me what you feel is going wrong with your relationship', Wendy stopped everything, turned to me and said, "So, are you going to tell her about your *hobby,* or am I?"

All of a sudden it got a lot warmer in the room. But I began. "Well, you see…um…all my life, I've wanted to dress in women's clothes," I stammered, looking away.

Then Wendy inserted, "And now you're running off to Detroit and Cleveland, spending our money, a thousand dollars, and taking all kinds of ridiculous chances, and for what? *What?* Can you tell me?"

Wendy liked to control conversations. The therapist looked like she'd been expecting Ward and June Cleaver and instead gotten John Wayne Gacy and spouse. Her face actually changed color, from pink to mostly white, in a heartbeat.

The therapist dove in, determined to navigate the unfamiliar waters into which we'd thrown her. "Well, that's an important thing for you both to know", she stammered.

After that, I recall little. She was stuck between Wendy's enormous anger and my reluctance to talk about the topic. We never got to sex change and I would have denied any interest in it if she had. The counselor tried bravely to stick to the issue, improving our relationship, but after two or three sessions we stopped going. Mostly, if memory serves me, because I had to get back to work in Toledo and Wendy back to work in Cincinnati. I thought it was stupid to begin any therapy in Dayton, but then I had a much better idea of how extensive the 'problem' really was.

One very positive aspect of that summer was that I began to get involved with the drum and bugle corps activity again. I had arranged to begin the testing involved in becoming a music judge. I felt I had all the qualifications they would want: former marching member, music degrees, and professional accomplishments. They arranged for me to trial judge three or four contests that summer so they could evaluate my comments about each group. They were screening for competence, wanting to know if I heard what most of the other music judges heard. They also screened me for bias: did I tend to favor the group I used to march with? And they screened my work for generally acceptable English and diction, for each judge makes their comments into a tape recorder during the group's performance so each corps' instructors can understand the commentary as it relates to the exact portion of the show in question. I passed all the tests quite easily.

I also became acquainted with the local Toledo drum corps and its music staff of one. That one, Dave, quickly became a friend and during that summer asked me to join their staff as a brass teacher. I declined, mostly because of the home situation, but also because I'd taken the judging road and felt I should not desert it.

◆   ◆   ◆

Wendy suggested, and I agreed, that I should start seeing a private therapist that fall. I let my fingers do the walking and called one with offices nearby. One cannot, of course, actually *call* a therapist. One can only *receive* a call from a therapist. One calls their person who gives them your message and the professional calls you back.

The therapist I called, after introducing himself and saying he was returning my call, asked me how I got his number. He seemed quite shocked that I would just pick a name out of the phone book. I had no idea that was not the usual way of choosing someone. We set an appointment anyway.

What a confusing year it had been up to that point: my father died in August of 1990 and from then on I'd been in a whirlwind culminating in coming out to myself as (at least) a cross dresser, telling my spouse about it, buying a house in Toledo, entering marriage counseling, and then private therapy. A very large part of me just wanted my life back. In fact, that was the way I phrased my situation to my new therapist. The Doctor asked me early on what I wanted to accomplish from my therapeutic time with him.

"I just want this all to go away," I said. I do not recall his exact response, but my memory of it was that it was akin to 'I can help you do that."

A few short years before I seemed to be normal, even to myself. My gender issues were there but not boiling over. As I thought back to those times, I began to think it was busyness that kept me sane, kept me whole, and that my problems of late were due to having too much free time. So when Dave again asked me to join the staff of the Glassmen in the fall of 1991, I did not have to think about it for very long. I took the job.

The Glassmen was great for me. It was a huge time commitment in addition to being the kind of all-consuming activity similar to the orchestra. When I was not practicing or working in the symphony I could be working on Glassmen things. And during the summers, when the orchestra was silent, I could be out on the road with the drum corps where 24 daily hours of my time was prescribed. Travel, sleep, eat, rehearse, and perform: that was the daily schedule from mid-June through mid-August. I loved it.

Wendy felt quite differently about it. She lamented my absences, both for herself and for Betty. I paid lip service to her feelings and hid behind the need for more income. She rightly pointed out that if you amortized the Glassmen salary over the hours worked I was working for pennies an hour, and that if money really was the issue I'd earn more flipping burgers.

I've learned many things in my life and one big one is that I had an enormous capacity to lie to myself. It did not make me a better liar in that Wendy always seemed to know when I was doing it, but it often worked for me. I had long before learned to compartmentalize in a way that allowed me to have my cake and eat it too. But like all crazy-making mental strategies the breakdown is inevitable.

◆   ◆   ◆

In therapy we worked on a behavior modification model for treatment. I admitted that I thought of men sexually. Not any individual men but rather men in general as potential sex partners. He never asked me if I saw myself as a woman and I never offered. His prescription was that whenever the urge to masturbate came upon me, I was to think exclusively of women. At 31 I had a healthy male body, so the need for release arose (so to speak) on a regular basis. I found it possible to follow his instructions, but it was quite boring and aside from ending successfully, also found it completely unsatisfying. In fact I generally loathed masturbating, but knew no way to end the need for it. My dislike for self-stimulation was exceeded only by my lack of desire for my wife. At that point in the fall of 1991, I was quite content to roll over and go to sleep on those infrequent nights when she was in residence in Toledo.

We'd bought a bigger home, a duplex, over the summer. But big young stupid fools that we were we did not have the house inspected as well as we should have. We got it for a great price or so it seemed: $18,000. I've often since joked that we paid $17,000 too much. It needed everything: roof, gutters, a furnace, a complete bathroom, and extensive interior repair. Within 5 years we'd replaced both furnaces, both water heaters, and most of the plumbing. Very quickly, we got 'upside down' on that house; we owed more on it than it was worth.

The work, some of which we hired out, was done piecemeal. My portion, interior repair, took a great deal of my free time. That was good. In the fall of '91, I'd not yet decided to purge my wardrobe. I kept it in the attic where I mistakenly thought Wendy would not find it. But she did and was quite upset, thinking I was in counseling to stop all that. I wanted to stop and I meant to stop, but after so many years of having the desire, the enormous need to dress and having no outlet for it, I was very reluctant to throw all the clothes away. After beginning therapy I rarely dressed again. But until I decided to purge I took a measure of comfort from knowing the clothes were there if I wanted them. So, having a great deal of home repair kept me busy and helped as I dealt with my gender issues.

That season of 91/92 was also my final chance to earn tenure in the orchestra. Tenure in an orchestra, as in academia, is awarded to players to prevent capricious firings by management or conductors. If management wants to fire a tenured player they must go though a longer and more drawn out process which usually favors the musician. I knew I was auditioning each time I picked up my horn.

The big work on the season, the one that was most exposed for first horn, was the 6th Symphony by Gustav Mahler. My colleague and our principal horn player Lowell Greer was due to be out of town that week, so I was scheduled to play that fabulous and famous work. I prepared for weeks ahead of time (all the while still playing in the orchestra daily) by creating technical studies out of the more difficult passages in the Mahler. When November came and it was time to do it, I felt I'd never been more prepared to both rehearse and perform a work.

Sometimes, a player is confident of their ability to perform a work, but they may fail to take the rehearsals into account. Rehearsals can be much more difficult than the performance because passages get played many times. Endurance is more of a factor in rehearsal. Also, professionals must be prepared to modify what they're doing to accommodate the other players in the orchestra, specifically the woodwinds for whom pitch adjustment is more difficult.

To say I nailed it would be an understatement. The principal trumpet player came up to me after that week was over and said he'd heard many performances by many horn players, but he'd never heard one as solid and convincing as the two I'd done on Mahler 6.

One funny incident: the conductor made the greatest faux pas a conductor can make. He praised me after the first of two performances saying, "Wow, Stewart, fantastic playing! I really felt like I could do anything I wanted and you'd be right there! Oops! Well, now, do it tomorrow, too." It's an old superstition that one should never compliment a horn player before all the performances are finished for fear of jinxing their playing. But I did as well the second night. I've never been particularly superstitious.

This is not to say the performances were flawless. But the errors were slight and seemingly inconsequential. Plus, I really believe the dynamic of the entire group that week was so positive. People were primed to hear what I was doing in a very positive light. Even to this day the solo from the slow movement sounds, to me, so beautiful when I hear it on the archival CD. It's almost hard to believe it's me.

In the remainder of that season we did other difficult and tricky works, but after Mahler 6 the conductor seemed to relax when I played first and I felt confident that tenure was mine. I was right.

Success has always had a way of seducing me. In high school it was sports. As long as I was busy with sports and seen as somewhat successful, I became that person, the successful sportsman. In early college, it was musical theater. I adopted that persona and busied myself with that hobby. Later in college I joined the Blue Devils and was for three years consumed with the excellence we achieved there. After college I went to work, and for 16 of 18 months I desired to be a good and well-paid insurance agent. But soon I knew my heart really was in music and I drifted back to what I loved. Graduate school was an adventure and while my gender issues were beginning to become more bothersome, I used my desire to achieve to help bury my problems in horn practice.

After using sexuality to hide from myself I settled on Wendy and once we were married, I suffered with the gender issues in an increasing way until that hectic year of 1991. The breakthrough I had then was really more of a breakout, caused by years of denial and repression. Faced with the choice to explore those issues more thoroughly, or learn a new set of coping skills in order to keep being Stewart, the horn player, husband, and father, I chose to remain as unchanged as possible.

Like in the past, I needed an all-consuming activity to keep me on the 'straight' track. But since I'd let the gender genie out of the bottle, I needed to work far harder at putting it back. One of the best tools I had was the orchestra itself. Mahler's 6th Symphony represented a real breakthrough in my horn playing, and I so much wanted to be good; to judge myself excellent and to know others did so as well. It was as if my entire existence relied on the attainment of that goal. I also needed the work on the house and the work with the Glassmen to keep me from slipping back into total gender hell.

These were not conscious decisions. I did not go for a long walk thinking, 'If I don't get more and more work I just know I'll dress.' I simply took the path of least resistance. My taking on of more work involved far less resistance than exploring my very obvious and painful gender issues. And my therapist was quite willing to employ his pet prescriptions of behavioral modification techniques.

As I look back on the years 92-96, I can see that I began them in a fog and ended them with even more confusion, and also a foreboding sense that things would not end well. For as I employed even more radical and drastic measures to repress my own core inner being, my mind began to push me in ways I never thought possible. I was torturing it, so it tortured right back.

In the 93/94 season Wendy decided we needed to move out to the rural countryside in order to have her horses right on the property with us. I objected, stating my belief that we did not have the income to own property in that area and also have resident horses as an affordable hobby. She countered that we needed to move to a 'decent' neighborhood anyway and she was going to find a place that would not cost any more than a standard house in a good school district. And she did just that.

However, the place was literally falling down around its own foundation. We closed in October of 1993, and for the next 9 months we paid two mortgages while a slew of contractors re-built that thing from the sill plates up. We also had to drive there (25 miles one way) twice a day to feed and water the horses, which she brought up right after the closing. Some days Wendy was out of town, and then I had to make those drives.

I began to greatly resent those horses. Wendy, I believe, felt completely justified in having them (only 3 at that time) in that she stayed with me even though

I gave her cause to divorce. I lost every discussion (quickly turned argument) we ever had about the horses. She maintained they paid for themselves through the foals she bred. I maintained that they cost us month after month. She did sell some over the years, maybe 3 or 4 foals for a total of $4000 or so. But I was sure our expenses were at least $2000 a year given hay at $2-$3 a bale (they ate at least 100-200 bales a year depending on size of herd) plus the vet and Ferrier bills. Of course, we also had to have a bigger car to haul the obligatory two-horse trailer. My disgust ran over, but I felt there was little I could say given that she was still with me.

Those 9 months after closing on the house and before we moved to Swanton encompassed the worst season I had with the orchestra before or since. I don't recall specific feelings of being trapped, but in looking back that's how I see it now. That was when I began to feel stuck in a place I did not like. That was the time when Wendy first started getting angry over our infrequent sexual relations. I was not open or honest about my resentment of the horses, not to mention so many other things. I was still in therapy, though each session involved me talking about my career (for that was far easier and more comfortable than discussing gender) and maybe getting around to answering his questions about how I was doing with 'the dressing thing' as he called it.

Lying has a way of deadening your soul. Nathanial Hawthorne said something like: 'No man can show one face to himself and another to the world without eventually becoming confused about which one is real.' I saw that engraved on a wall at his college, which the camera panned on an episode of *The Sopranos*. How appropriate! Tony Soprano and I had a lot in common. Many would, and do everyday, find it very easy to believe that the face shown to the world is obviously the real one. We're taught that from childhood. 'It's actions, not words', 'actions speak louder than words', 'the road to hell is paved with good intentions', and other aphorisms are designed to reinforce the idea that the person you are with others represents the real you. But it is my contention that people have a desire to be part of the group, so they twist themselves into a configuration that gets them accepted. In the case of Tony Soprano one gets the idea that Tony is a reluctant mobster, but even he's not yet aware that he loathes the mobster lifestyle. In my life, though a part of me was crying out for attention, I remained steadfast in my zeal to conceal as much of my soul as possible.

In the case of gender conflict, each dysphoria sufferer deals with that dilemma differently. Take the 'classic' transsexuals who from an early age understand that they are, despite physical attributes to the contrary, a girl or boy. I believe anyone who has done this to be a particularly strong willed individual. Think of it: a 5 to

10 year-old person willing to assert that what they think is correct when they have not only their whole family, but school, church, and society telling them the opposite. Somehow exceptional young transgendered people have been able to understand that one is not the sum total of what others perceive them to be. They know that we are self-determined creatures. Is it surprising that the vast majority of gender conflicted persons do their best to adapt their physical body?

The great sales professionals knew well that we are self-determined creatures. Earl Nightingale called it 'the strangest secret'. Sayings like 'You are what you think about most,' and 'Successful people do what failures don't like to do' really are true. It's the mind that has the power.

But of course, by accepting those sayings as truth a logical argument becomes obvious: why can't gender conflicted people simply change their minds? Why indeed. 'And why not,' I thought in 1993. Those positive thinking sales sayings I'd learned well in my youth were still there alive in my mind. In 1993 I began to apply them to my gender conflict.

The first problem was sex. I've painted a picture here of someone profoundly uninterested in sex. That is not quite the right picture. The essence of conflict is being pulled in two directions. My body was very much interested in sex. It was me—*my mind*—that wished for surcease from that drive. I think most men take that testosterone-driven desire for sex as being equal to their own, as if their *mind* was directing their *body* to have a sexual response to things (visual, verbal, olfactory, auditory, etc.) 15-50 times a day. It's quite the opposite. In men, the body really does have a mind of its own. The comic Robin Williams says men surely do have a brain and a penis, but only enough blood to operate one at a time. And I hated it when I went 'out of my mind'.

But I also went out of my mind numerous times a day. Shortly after I decided to purge my clothing collection I started to fantasize more about men sexually. I did not ask for those thoughts and I found no help from all of my behavior modification and positive thinking. *Driven to distraction* is an appropriate phrase. Eventually, I just had to know more. I'd taken my gender conflict and locked it away re-building the dam that had held those feelings in check until 1991. But the dam was a much weaker structure now. It had leaks. One was sexual drive.

'Why don't you just go home and schtup your wife, *stupid*,' I thought. Yes. Exactly. Why not? Well, there's the short answer and the long answer, but this book is all about long answers. The short answer was it was increasingly difficult to fake an interest I did not have. The long answer involves *why* I was not interested. People raised male are taught to be very concerned with sex, including its frequency, the number of and relative beauty of partners, and most important of all, its 'normalcy', meaning is it heterosexual sex and desire or not.

I really had no idea why I did not desire my wife. She was and is a beautiful person with great integrity and honesty. But with neither dressing nor honesty a part of my life, I once again became confused and began to believe I might truly be gay. I sought out a local gay bar. I went during the day hoping to not find anyone I already knew. I was lucky. Only about 8 guys were there. I wore my leather jacket over business slacks and a polo shirt. Since I'd only been in a gay bar one other time (except for *Caesar's* around the corner in 1991), and that was at midnight when it was packed, I was mildly surprised that every head turned on my entrance and did what I could only describe as a thorough checking out. I took a seat that had space open on both sides. I was not there to give anyone the impression that I wanted to go with them (though I did hope someone would approach me). It did not take long. An older man called out from his seat across the bar.

"You've never been in a place like this before," a flat statement. He'd read my nervousness.

"That's not true."

We talked for a while and he wrote his phone number and name on a scrap of paper. I left after 20 minutes. Is there a cheating response that men (or women) have to situations like that? I believed I loved my wife. I know now in hindsight and years of reflection that I did, and still do, love her. Though our relationship was flawed and rocky, I'd grown to love Wendy through our shared life, our baby, and our careers. But I was not a heterosexual man and could not give her what she needed. And what she certainly did not need was me getting AIDS and killing her! I knew from my body's response that I was interested in being with a man. Yet I could not. *Saying* no did not make it any easier to *believe* no. I continued to think about men.

I took solace from my confusion and desires in work. In addition to my duties with the symphony and my teaching job with The Glassmen I also taught private lessons to anyone who would pay. My studio size varied from 3 to 8 students. Private teaching was not only lucrative but an excellent way to improve my own playing. By listening to young players struggling with the same (or sometimes completely foreign) technical problems and attempting to find a workable solution for each student, I better understood the need for my own life-long learning. Only in times of great hubris have I felt like 'I'd arrived' and no longer needed to study the process of playing the horn.

The horn is a very unforgiving instrument. Compare it with the piano: on the piano there are 88 keys, and if you strike one of them you'll get that note every time. Pianists *do* have to contend with a *bazillion* notes in any given work, but getting any one note is not by any stretch of the imagination hard. However, on the horn, even playing a single note can take years to learn to do at all let alone properly. It's a very Zen-like process which I liken to golf.

In golf, the seemingly simple task of swinging the club and striking the ball is upon study inordinately difficult. And it's just so with the horn. Consider: one must coordinate air, lips, tongue, and all the muscles in between the stomach and the lips that can change the necessary balance. With too much lip, one gets a tight sound; too much air, airy and pushy sound; muscles too tight, poor endurance and range problems. Through teaching I learned to be a much better player. I often said to my students that I should be paying them. Fortunately none of their parents tried to take me up on that!

In the maelstrom of the 1993/1994 season, what with the two mortgages, and horses to feed and water through a 50 mile round trip twice daily, and questioning my technique, and everything else, one of our infrequent evenings of sex resulted in Wendy's second pregnancy. Bonnie was born two days after Christmas 1994, just about six months after we moved into the Swanton home.

I love my children more than my own life, a statement to which some have taken great exception given my choices. I'll be discussing that love and how I came to recognize it when I get to the dramatic events of 1999. But upon Bonnie's arrival, I could not have been more in love with both of my children. And Wendy was beautiful as well. There is something beyond lovely about a pregnant or nursing woman. They beam, *they glow,* they are the essence of life. Many of my favorite pictures of Wendy are from this time. I believe we both hoped (silly though it was) that Bonnie would revitalize our marriage.

So Wendy had the double glow of just having delivered one of God's gifts to the world and believing that she and I were on the short course to marital bliss. I was working and earning well. She was working as a musician in various regional orchestras as well as a regular extra with Toledo. I enjoyed having Wendy cover parts for us when we needed more than our regular compliment of players. Some works require up to 8 horns, or even 10 in the case of the Mahler 2nd symphony. Wendy was, and still is, one of my favorite horn players. Since our divorce and my transition having her assist me on the first part has become too awkward for me to handle, so I've stopped calling her for those jobs. But anytime we need a section player she's high on the list.

For a couple of years, from the move to Swanton until 1996 when I went to work in the symphony office, Wendy and I enjoyed our best time together. We were on the same page about so many things, from horn playing to child rearing to money. Though we remained at odds over sex, I was able to rouse myself to some regularity of duty, enough to keep her from being too angry too often.

Wendy made up little musical motifs for each child. Betty had hers and Bonnie's was a variant on Betty's. So every night when I arrived home I'd whistle the two motifs one after the other. I also would use them in random improvisations while doing chores; taking the intervals and elaborating on them. I learned that from Wendy.

We reaffirmed our commitment to having Wendy home with the girls. She offered to go get a day job but we both truly felt it best for the kids to spend as much time with a parent as possible. If more money was needed I volunteered to produce it, making Wendy's near complete commitment (aside from some evening horn jobs) to the children possible. It was a win/win situation for both of us. She got to do what we wanted: stay home with her beautiful daughters. And I got to go out and earn the bread. That helped me in more ways than one! Not only did it keep me busy and tired, but filling that traditional kind of male role served to reaffirm my identity and simultaneously dug my trap deeper as well.

In 1995 I was offered a position as development director for The Glassmen. This job required that I seek out and secure new sources of funding for the group, meet high-powered local business leaders, and make the case for their support of the Glassmen. I thought in all honesty that that was just the kind of job I could do. I could not have been more wrong. When one has denied strong personal truths it's not a long stretch to believe one has qualities one does not. That job required a kind of glad-handing, back slapping, easy friendliness that I found increasingly difficult to act out. My need to work harder increased, both due to the necessity to earn more and to help me maintain my carefully crafted persona, and in that sense the additional job was great. I was busy morning to night.

I attacked the job with vigor. The first step was to finally become computer literate, something I'd been loath to do. I learned about press releases, boards of directors, and many other things. But what I did not figure out until I'd already failed was that I needed to be meeting 5 to 10 of those high-powered business people every week.

I went to some social events, chamber of commerce meetings, and did meet some influential people, but nowhere near the number I should have. I secured no new sources of funding for the Glassmen. My biggest coup was getting a local current affairs television program, *The Editors,* to do an entire show on The Glassmen. One marching member and I were the guests. This was a major deal and did attract some additional interest from the community, but 1996 was also the first year we were without the executive director who'd gotten us to where we were. He was lured away to become the boss of the entire drum corps organization, Drum Corps International, after 10 totally successful years with the Glassmen. So we were dealing with an interim director and a staff that never really worked that well together. We soon learned how much we'd all relied on Dan (the former director) to keep us cordial. 1996 ended with us dropping to 13th place (from 8th in 1995).

When The Glassmen hired a new director in the fall of 1996 I put in a call to him. I intended to resign from both my teaching and my administrative duties but he subscribed to what I've come to facetiously call 'the modern business ethic'. He did not return calls from people to whom he did not want to talk. So I never got fired and I never got the chance to quit in person. Eventually, after waiting 8 or 9 weeks for a call, I wrote him a letter of resignation, something that seemed silly since it was painfully obvious that he wanted nothing to do with me.

Fortunately, though the Glassmen door closed another opened. The Toledo Symphony asked me to join their office staff in a sales capacity. I'd learned that the kind of perpetually happy demeanor one needed for development was not quite the same as the situational acting that sales people must employ. By 1996 I was aware that I was not temperamentally suited to sustained bouts of bonhomie, but I could manage a sales encounter.

8

Dark Clouds on the Horizon

In 1996 a greater sense of disconnectedness than I had yet felt began to come over me. Perhaps it was the demise of my job with the Glassmen. More likely it was the toll that denial and lying was taking on my psyche.

Upon leaving the Glassmen I went to work in the marketing department of the Toledo Symphony. At first they did not know what to do with me. The tickets were sold primarily by subscription and through newspaper and radio ads. Other people handled such tasks as selling advertising in the program book and selling the entire orchestra to outside presenters (churches and performing arts series in other towns). So I began to build databases. I manually entered every church found in three area phone books; over 1000 entries. Every college and university music department faculty member got fed into the database; well over 600 entries. I did the same for all the high school music programs and listings of area private teachers.

Once that was done I began to think up ways of filling the numerous empty seats the symphony played to on our classics series. I initiated a program to give tickets to the Boys and Girls clubs, the youth groups at the YMCA, and anyone else who would take them. I discovered that the old and famous adage 'you can't give them away' is old and famous for a reason.

I also spent a great deal of time trying to get high school music programs to take on a particular performance night at the symphony and sell tickets to their families for a profit. It was an *Amway* kind of multi-level marketing scheme. We agreed to provide excellent seats to the music programs at a low cost—$5 or $10—and the band could sell them for whatever they wanted. We suggested they sell them at just less than the price the symphony charged for the same seat. Every band director I spoke with thought it was a great idea except for one thing: they didn't believe the families would pay $5 per seat let alone $25 or so. A few took on the program and sadly, each proved that the cynics and pessimists were indeed correct. Why pay to go to the symphony when you can stay home and see free reruns of *Married With Children*? But the best part for me was that I had a goal. I felt somewhat responsible for filling the seats at our concerts, even though we had a marketing director whose job it was to do that very thing

I truly loved to spend time with my children. We routinely went to the local playground for swings and slides and the other fun things. Reading to them was a looked forward to affair for us all on those evenings when I was home, and a regular occurrence if I was home during the day. But the Toledo Symphony, like quite a number of regional and metropolitan orchestras, rehearsed in the evening. I was away from home most evenings. What with the day job at the symphony office and evening rehearsals, I was usually gone from home from 8:30am to 11pm.

I felt most comfortable when in my chair in the symphony. Since my early college days, I'd dreamed of playing first horn at the professional level, and I was doing it. I'd come to rely more and more on my symphony position for role confirmation. Each good rehearsal and performance reinforced my male identity. Each problematic day or period caused me intense pain as I felt I was not only disappointing my colleagues but also jeopardizing my entire persona. I routinely blew small problems way out of proportion and downplayed the beautiful and successful things I was doing. That is the trademark of a person fundamentally ashamed of whom they are: whatever goes right is luck or not that big of a deal, whatever goes wrong is evidence that the core feelings of shame are correct.

Being a neurotic (taking more responsibility for things than is actually warranted) actually made improvement on the horn more possible. I was terribly critical of my own work. I listened to all of our concerts through the archived recordings. If I heard an intonation problem anywhere in the group and I was playing at the time I mentally took the blame. I became much more aware of my own pitch tendencies and problems.

I continued to learn about the process of playing the horn, analyzing in detail as many aspects of technique as I could in order to have them become automatic. When technique flows the player is able to simply create beautiful music instead of constantly monitoring him or herself as if they were a computer.

To fill more time, I resumed a regular running program I'd begun in 1992 (soon after entering therapy) but dropped when my workload got too demanding in 1995/96. I also organized a weekly pick-up basketball game amongst some of the guys in the symphony. We met weekly at a local church for almost a year. I was pretty awful but enjoyed running up and down the floor. It was always more fun to run with a purpose (get the ball, score, defense) than just hitting the pavement for exercise.

In January 1997 I was featured as soloist on our chamber orchestra series playing the 4th horn concerto by Mozart. That went so well I decided to put together a recital. I'd not played a full recital for years and enjoyed the intense focus on solo works. That recital also went very well so I decided to enter The American Horn Competition for summer 1997. It would be my third trip to that event over the years. I spent large numbers of hours practicing, including hiring a pianist to work with me, though she would not be my pianist at the competition. By working on the pieces with the piano parts I was better able to play in-tune as well as refine my musical phrasing ideas. My performance there was a quantum leap in solo work and I went home with the second prize.

The 97/98 symphony season was my first as the sole occupant of the principal horn chair. My mentor and teacher, Lowell Greer, was no longer there to share the load. I was both sad and thrilled. I missed my friend and felt bad for the way he'd been treated, but the fact was I was still there and had the chair to myself. This forced me to refine my practice routines. I added more strength and flexibility drills. Daily, I played a crescendo-decrescendo (get louder-get softer) exercise that encompassed three entire octaves. I regularly played a 20-30 minute long tone study that helped with tone, intonation, and endurance. All this paid off as I was rarely caught short in my work in that season or the next.

Wendy and I seemed to be humming along, each of us busy with work, our pet projects, and focused on the children for regular intervals daily. But as bedtime came every day I continued to find it difficult to initiate physical intimacy. I loved spooning as we fell asleep, or just reaching out and falling asleep with my hand touching her, but getting worked up for sex was next to impossible. I could manage by giving her a massage. Through prolonged touching, I knew that eventually my body would respond and I'd be able to give her what she wanted and needed. I never minded the feeling of orgasm, it was the foreplay and the sexual role of the male against which I chafed.

I'd been invited by one of the American Horn Competition judges to play a recital at his late spring horn weekend in the mountains outside Albuquerque New Mexico. The preparation for that led to a fun and enjoyable time where I met some more horn players from the west.

As the summer of 1998 approached I proposed that the symphony management hire me to run a subscription telemarketing program. For years the symphony had no organized effort at selling new subscriptions via the telephone. I'd done some telemarketing for magazine subscriptions just before moving to Cincinnati in 1984 and more importantly, had secured all of my insurance sales appointments through cold calling in 1982 and '83.

Most professional arts marketing firms will charge 50-60% of the gross to run a phone campaign. My offer to the TSO was that we pay $8 per hour and a straight 10% commission to the phone callers, plus a generous bonus structure designed to keep them there and on the job for the whole 9 weeks. For myself I asked for only 5% of all sales. By my estimates our costs would be 35-40%; well below the 'professionals' in large part because I was willing to work for so little. Since I had little experience and no history from which to work I had absolutely no idea how well we'd do, but I had a hunch that given a polite and pointed script (though I much preferred the callers extemporize) we would be able to make sales. I was right. In 9 weeks, 6 of us sold over $35,000 of new and renewal subscriptions. And best of all our cost factor was actually about 25%, well under my estimate. To say the management was thrilled would be an understatement!

My stock had never been higher. They thought I played very well and was really becoming worth their money in the office. I'd always thrived on the good will and praise of others and the sense of worth I derived from that was a big help.

I parlayed the New Mexico recital into a performance of the same music at San Jose State, my alma mater, in the fall of 1998. That trip also produced the bonus of having a number of old friends from high school and The Blue Devils in the audience. We all went out for good beer at Gordon Biersch after the performance.

After my California recital I got down to the work of the symphony season. We had a great line up that year, including the Shostakovich Cello Concerto with the legendary Russian Cellist Rostropovich as soloist. On his previous visit in 1997 he'd played the Dvorak concerto, which has a wonderful moment early in the work for solo horn. I was later told by one of his former musicians in the National Symphony that he rarely asks the horn player to stand at the conclusion of his Dvorak performances, but he'd asked me to stand back in 1997, which was a rare honor indeed. For his second performance in 1998 he chose the Shostakovich, which has an even larger role for the first horn.

Thanksgiving of 1998 found us in Kentucky visiting Wendy's mother and stepfather, two of my favorite people in the whole world. Over the years I found them to be kind hearted and genuinely loving people to Wendy, the girls, and myself. But Thanksgiving weekend was also a performance weekend for the symphony so we'd traveled down separately. Friday morning I headed back to Toledo for an evening rehearsal.

About halfway home I began to see myself, to see me at some future date, but as a woman. To this day I have no idea why *then,* why at *that* time those images and thoughts came back. But when they did they would not leave. I played the radio, I rolled down the window, I stopped and walked around, and I sang out loud at the top of my lungs. Nothing I did could banish the cross gendered thoughts from my mind.

Over the years I'd expended a great deal of energy in constructing a credible and serviceable male persona for myself. And there I was worse off with the issue than I'd ever been! I got physically angry and quite agitated. 'God dammit,' I thought, 'what the *fuck* is going on!?'

I was so disturbed that as I passed a grocery store in suburban Toledo, I stopped and used my sure-fire method for buying pantyhose. I hated myself for my weakness. I'd not bought anything since 1991. Here I was absolutely on top of the world; recent international music competition prizewinner, noted recitalist, successful businessman, and respected hornist with the Toledo Symphony…and I'm buying pantyhose to wear under my wife's clothes.

"What a fuckin' freak, you are," I said to myself over and over again. But I did buy them, and wear them. It was almost as if I could hear my father's voice. Any self-criticism came in his voice. Not because he ever criticized me (because he did not), but more because I believe I was afraid he *would* if he'd ever found out certain truths about me.

I was alone in the house that Thanksgiving weekend. Wendy and the girls stayed in Kentucky until Monday. Wendy still had that great green sweater dress I'd borrowed in 1989 so I wore that along with numerous others. I walked around the entire house and at night even walked to the barn dressed in spite of the big safety light illuminating the entire yard.

From time to time I'd pass a mirror. 'Wow,' I'd think, 'could I really do this?' 'This' meant transition, but I could not let my mind go there. I'd always stopped short of admitting that I wished I'd been born a girl. I did not allow myself to think further. I didn't even desire to masturbate anymore. I just liked wearing the clothes so much. I hated it when I had to go to rehearsals or concerts. I was distracted and irritable all weekend.

That sense of distractedness and irritability was the first sign of a massive depression that fell over me beginning on that weekend. I've often asked myself if I somehow did it to myself, caused the gender problem, but I do believe it was simply a lifetime of feelings, thoughts, and needs that I'd kept locked away. The dam holding back those thoughts and feelings broke for good. It was that weekend that my psyche put me on notice saying 'I will not be ignored any longer!'

The very next weekend was the special concert with Rostropovich and the Shostakovich concerto. I'd been quite disturbed through that whole week by my regression the previous weekend. I thought constantly of clothing and being a woman. It was very, very tiring. But I had to deliver for Rostropovich. I once again impressed the great man enough for him to bring me to the front of the stage at the conclusion of the work for a solo bow next to him. As usual, I was both pleased and embarrassed simultaneously.

1999 dawned with me being increasingly distracted by my 'condition'. This was the depression that nearly killed me. I floundered around like a drowning man and grasped for the familiar lifesavers that had kept my head above water for years. In the early 90s, I used work to distract myself. In '99 I had all the work I could get and handle. So I decided that I would organize a concert to honor a little known American composer, Alec Wilder. He was perhaps most famous for writing popular songs for singers like Frank Sinatra, Mabel Mercer, and Tony Bennett. But he also wrote a great deal of concert music for 'classical' instruments, much of it crafty and cute with wonderful melodies and jazz-type harmonies.

I talked a local singer into learning (read: memorizing!) ten of Wilder's better jazz/popular songs and convinced three local jazz musicians to back him up, including a wonderful pianist who devised clever arrangements. The concert opened with a 15-member flute choir, followed by a trio for horn, tuba and piano performed by members of the Tower Brass Quintet and a local pianist. The first half closed with 5 of the 10 songs by the jazz group. The second half opened with three works for solo instruments and a string orchestra of volunteers from the Toledo Symphony. We performed the Air for Flute, Suite for Horn and Strings, and Suite No. 2 for Tenor Sax and Strings. The concert concluded with the final 5 songs. We attracted about 150 people who paid $5 each. The local classical music reviewer wrote a preview article as well as a review. The local public radio station recorded the concert for later broadcast. I even talked them into featuring me as the on-air host of the program.

The Wilder concert was to take place in late May of 1999. I knew as we got within a few weeks of the performance that something was definitely wrong with me. I was sleeping very little and eating even less. I'd been able to reconstruct some of my self-control and was no longer doing any dressing, but instead driving myself to complete distraction with projects, exercise, and work.

I spent months planning the concert including securing the music, paying performance rites, and paying rental fees. I learned an entire new computer program, *Pagemaker*, just to be able to create the program booklet. As the concert was finishing and Doug Nichol was singing the last song of the evening, the beautiful and poignant *South To A Warmer Place*, a huge emptiness in my soul became apparent. This effort, this project, had not filled up the empty place in me. It was fun. It was even rewarding and worth doing, though it cost me over $500 out of my pocket. But the unstated unacknowledged goal had not been met. I was still depressed. It was a long and lonely drive home.

The completion of the Wilder event coincided with the end of the symphony season. The summer telemarketing program would not begin until July. Though I'd always been wary of free time, for the first time in my life I was actually afraid of all the relatively free time yawning before me.

9

The Hell Of Depression

For months I'd planned on taking my older daughter to visit my mother in Las Vegas that June. It was all I could do to drag myself through the trip. Photos from the trip show me droopy eyed and slow looking. Betty, though, seemed to have a great time, especially on our short trip to the Grand Canyon.

In the final weeks of June I found myself sitting in my office and staring into the wall. No thought. A wisp of thought would break through, but I did not want it. Whatever mental activity there was I had to push down again. It was during this time that I first began to seriously entertain the idea of suicide. I was in pain and it was becoming physical. There was no definite ache, no certain spot to which I could point. I just had a huge sense of *heaviness*. I could only drag through my days.

I began to play suicide scenes in my mind: rope (flunked boy scouts), knife (never!), jump off the high level bridge (quick, but scary on the way down), slit wrists (a woman's way, better not go there...). I settled on using a gun and pondered where to fire the bullet. I knew I would put the barrel in my mouth, but where would I *be* when I did it? I had terrible visions of traumatizing my unsuspecting children. I hated the thought of inflicting that kind of memory on anyone let alone my family. But since I had to do it somewhere, and I had to be found for Wendy to collect on the life insurance, her barn seemed the best choice. Then I worried about someone finding the gun before Wendy found me and getting hurt, so I decided I'd have just one bullet. That way, after it was over the gun would be useless.

One particular day I decided it was time. I would go from lunch to the gun store. 'But,' I thought, 'I'd better stop at the office. I'd hate for people to think I didn't do my job. I need to check my voice mail once more before I go. I'm expecting some customers to call.'

106

I went to the office so that once I was dead everyone would say what a wonderful person I'd been. I found six messages on my machine. I'd not had more that one or two a day for weeks!

'Well, I guess I'd better deal with all these before I go,' I thought. And by the time I'd dealt with them it was 5:30pm, the gun store was closed, and I had to go home. The intense need to do away with myself subsided for the rest of that evening, though that feeling of having slid to the bottom of an un-climbable hill would return on numerous other occasions.

Perhaps what disturbed me most was that the feelings of femininity were much clearer than in 1991. Many times over the previous 8 years I recalled my month's long episode in 1991. The thoughts would sneak up on me at odd times and I found myself smiling, remembering not just the way I'd dressed, or my (only imagined) pretty reflection in the mirror, but seeing the way people would treat a woman (me—in my dream); they held doors, smiled as I approached a clerk, and said "yes ma'am, may I help you?" After a few moments of slipping away to that fantasy, I'd jolt back to reality and stuff those thoughts away like so many second hand skirts in a garbage bag.

So when I had thoughts of being a woman during Thanksgiving '98, *of wishing I were a woman,* they were not my first thoughts of this since 1991. Oh no! But it was the first time since 1991 that I had *no* success putting them back in 'their place'. I've read about other transsexuals since I first read *Second Serve,* in books and over the internet, and nearly all have the same core elements in common: cross gender feelings that range from mild to intense growing stronger over time, a period of 'stuffing' where the sufferer denies or represses the unwanted thoughts, a period of *intense* suffering where they find they can no longer deal with the stuffing, lying, or denial, but also cannot yet deal with the truth about themselves (this is the time most likely to lead to suicide), and finally a decision to seek some kind of help.

In the summer of 1999 I lost all hope that I would ever be free of this. It was always hope and wishing that I'd be just a regular guy that made it possible for me to keep going. I looked back and could see that I truly expected my gender identity to solidify as male. Instead it was in a continual metamorphosis.

I wanted to stand out for my horn playing, for my parenting, and other 'acceptable' things. I heard the late night comics ridicule anyone not mainstream, or worse, not interested in abiding by the standards of the mainstream. I'd been able to get as far as I had through fairly strict thought control, allowing only the kinds of thoughts that would propel me toward my goals. I knew I'd not been completely successful at it, but did not know what I'd do without that ability to compartmentalize my gender conflict. It was a hard truth to swallow, that I was not normal in the way I'd always defined it.

A few days later I stopped into a gay bar to pick up a local 'what's happening' newspaper. I knew there would be some kind of hotline or address for transsexual support. I found only a P.O. Box address. I wrote asking for help as soon as possible and left my number. Candy called me a few days later. She offered to meet me anywhere I was comfortable. I let her choose and we met at *Blu Jeans*, a local lesbian bar. Candy was even taller than me; 6'5" at least though not fat. I felt small in her presence.

It's strange how, though I'm tall, I've never felt big. I've taken the fact of looking down on people (literally) as a matter of course but never taken on the persona of someone who's big and powerful. Perhaps my 'issues' made me profoundly uncomfortable with taking my male act that far.

It is quite common for men suffering with GID to fly into what's known as hyper masculinity. This is where they become soldiers, firemen, athletes; any cloak of manhood that will help the world see them as they wish to be seen. Both male and female GID sufferers (male far more than female) run to traditional roles as a guise, all in the hopes that saying it will make it so; that acting like a man and being treated like a man will make them feel like a man. I'd never been able to go that far with my act aside from my 'Don Juan' phase in the mid 80s.

Candy asked me the standard questions: How long have you felt this way, have you ever cross-dressed, how old were you when you first started this, ever gone out in public cross-dressed, and other general questions. I felt great, *it felt great*, to be talking to a real live transsexual and the time passed very quickly. I asked her if she would shop with me. I wanted to buy some more clothes, but I also wanted to see how people viewed *her*. I felt bad about seeing a masculine body when I looked at her, but wondered if perhaps it was my prior knowledge that colored my eyes.

I met her a week later to shop at some second hand stores. I was quite disappointed to see dozens of people staring at her openly and with undisguised smirks on their faces. I believe people are taught to do this by their peers. We look down on others in order to feel good about ourselves. No one is easier to look down upon than a visibly transgendered person. 'Hell, they don't know if they're a guy or a girl,' a person may think. And that thought gives them great comfort. They can then say to themselves: 'at least I know what I am.' So when someone sees a gender variant person their disgust is tinged with thanks. Thanks that the person is both there (to help make them feel better), but also that they're not one of them.

Candy was a wonder! I knew she was aware of the stares, but she was confident in herself. "I *know* who I am," she'd often say, with emphasis on the *know*. What an example to us all. There is no other class of person in the US so openly ridiculed and looked down upon as the visibly gender variant person. Yet she had great respect for herself and conducted herself through life with an enviable personal dignity that anyone would be lucky to possess.

Candy helped me pick out a few things. At her favorite wig shop I bought a decent wig, though as always I hated the look and feel of them. The clerk there was very kind, she'd known Candy for years.

Candy also gave me the name and number of an experienced gender therapist, someone who specialized in treating persons with gender dysphoria (i.e.: transsexuals). I was still very confused about the whole issue. Though I was willing to buy clothes again after an 8-year denial, I was still not ready to think the issue completely through. I *wanted* to be a man! I had a family and a career. Though I knew I was in a poor marriage, I loved (and still love!) my children. My career was and is a source of unending pleasure and reward. So to contemplate what my mind was attempting to force me to face was still too much. But I was eager to talk. I made an appointment with Michelle Clossick, the gender therapist.

For the first time in my life, I began to write in a journal; not so much out of curiosity, but out of extreme pain. I found that putting pen to paper temporarily relieved some of the worst aspects of depression. I felt I was actually doing something; taking some positive action on my own behalf. Here are some writings from those first few days of journaling.

7/28/99

I've always wondered whether the proper perspective can be achieved. Do I see what I want to see, or expect to see, because I'm thinking through the cross-gender filter, or can I truly be objective and see the reality of my life, remembering events and thoughts as they truly were? Once I settled in Toledo while Wendy lived in Cincinnati most of the time, I had many more thoughts of dressing. I got bolder. I shopped at K-mart and Payless Shoes. I developed a collection. I cannot say I got very good at it. I still saw a man when I looked in the mirror, but I felt good while dressed. I felt awful when I had to take it off. I both wanted to dress more and stop altogether. Both thoughts existing at the same time…*Both thoughts*. Still, 8 years later—**both thoughts!** But much more complicated.

Is it always better to choose life? Would not my family be better served by the $350,000 insurance money than by some freak of a father who wears women's clothes, embarrasses the poor kids at school, and is not even resident in the same house with his own children? Why do I want to escape from masculinity? Wendy would say I just want to duck responsibility: kids, job, etc. That's why it's all coming out now.

7/29/99

Nobody can make it go away. Nobody can make living with this easy. How will I get out of the house and what will I do? The whole idea is the cross-gendered expression—*expression* being the key word. In order for something to be expressed it has to be out in the world.

I met Michelle for the first time in August of 1999. In that first hour I detailed as much of my history as I could. During my previous therapy I'd lied (to myself and hence to the Doctor), withheld information, put spin on various things, and did an all around good job of faking a life. With Michelle I held back nothing.

As we wrapped up our 50 minutes I asked her what she thought was in store for me. She sighed, paused and looked up, "A monumental amount of change," was all she was willing to then offer.

We met weekly at first, then twice a month after the first 3 sessions. As the symphony season began to resume in early September, I recall feeling like my old self. My suicidal thoughts had gone and I felt like the in-control guy I'd been accustomed to feeling for quite a number of years. Around that time Michelle asked me to take the Burns depression test. I figured that since I was better I'd answer the questions based on how I'd felt at my worst: over the summer. I scored a 74, which is well nigh dead. I then answered the questions based on how I felt at that moment, September 1999, *which was how I remembered feeling for years*. I scored a 26, which is still fairly depressed. I was quite shocked. I'd been depressed for years! 'And over what,' I thought. Then I remembered that I'd been hiding and repressing something important for many, many years.

This information served to burst my bubble a little. I was still resisting change. Even though I was honest with Michelle and told her every awful detail of my life, I wanted my created life, the one I'd been trying to live for 40 years, not the life of a freak, which is what I saw for myself if I attempted transition. I had few if any memories of seeing any women over 6 feet tall, let alone seeing any weighing close to 200 pounds. I thought I'd be extremely ugly and immediately recognized as a gender freak wherever I went. I just wanted to be 'normal'. I'd tried so hard to be normal, to be the guy the world thought, *and I thought,* I was and should be.

As November arrived I began to slump down again into the hellish nightmare of suicidal depression. That month we were scheduled to perform the Symphony No. 1 by Gustav Mahler. I recall feeling like every note I played was shit; too loud, out of tune, not a pretty sound. I was sleeping very poorly, eating sporadically, and losing weight as well. My memory of the performances was of terror alternating with disgust. Terror at what was coming next and disgust with what did. In 2002, after I was transitioned and living full time as Sandra, I pulled the archival CD to hear those performances. I heard none of the problems I'd thought I'd had. It was not my best work but it was far from my worst, and quite acceptable over all. That's an example of what depression will do to one's sense of self.

November gave way to December and my depression grew. Wendy was pressing me for some answers. She knew I'd re-entered therapy but had no idea why, other than what seemed to her a mild case of depression. I'd not told her of feeling suicidal nor of the resumption of private dressing. In fact, I discarded all the things I'd purchased while shopping with Candy once the symphony season began and my false sense of recovery came over me. I was hiding from everyone again, including myself. I was only able to approach the truth a little at a time. At each session with Michelle, we'd chip into it a little more.

"What do you feel like when you dress," she asked. There were many other questions. We discussed my birth family and childhood home life, from the taunting and teasing I suffered, through the problems my sister had, to the sadness I felt at my mother not being interested in hearing my work as a professional musician; her not even being able to fake any interest.

I decided in December I had to tell Wendy something and the truth was the only thing she deserved. I'd decided nothing about my future or about any changes I might make in my life, so I could not tell her what was going to happen. As we drove back from one of her performances I began. She listened calmly with a not too surprised air about her. I was grateful for her kindness. She asked some questions, which were nearly the same questions she'd asked me in 1991.

"Do you want a sex change?" "How long have you felt this way?" And new since '91, "have you known since '91, but just didn't tell me?" I also told her of the suicidal depression and the death I had planned for myself for the previous summer. That truly shocked her. She told me I should proceed with reading, therapy, and whatever it took to help.

I began to openly read relevant books at home. Wendy looked them over as well. I brought her the Brown/Roundsley book *TrueSelves*, which is considered one of the best introductory books on the subject of transsexualism. We discussed our sex life, our children, and our future. Even the intimacy created by our honesty and sharing could not spark any sexual desire in me. The years of pretending coupled with the well known effects of depression on libido kept me mute on that topic. I believe she wanted, for the sake of the children, to save the marriage. But she also had needs as a person, needs that I had not fulfilled and was making it plain I either would not, or could not, fulfill in the future.

On New Year's Eve of 1999 she told me we would be divorcing. I'd just not allowed my thinking to contemplate divorce and was momentarily stunned. I got up from the table and wandered the house. In hindsight, it's the same kind of reaction I had when I'd tried to break up with Wendy. I believe that, like 1988, I so very much feared losing her as my shield, as my cover, that I lost all composure. I cried like I'd not done since that night 11 and a-half years before. I wailed, I railed, and I felt like dying. She asked if I was suicidal again and I nodded, unable to speak. Quietly and gently, she told me how much our children cared for me, and how much I would hurt them if I left them that way. I knew she was right, but I'd never hurt so badly in my entire life. A lifetime of illusions was ripped away in that instant. Ahead I saw only loneliness and a freakish future, and behind me only my own lies and denial. And to make matters worse, I had to put on my tux and head out to a New Year's Eve symphony job!

A good musician is at heart an accomplished actor. I did a masterful job of compartmentalizing to get through that evening. But on the way back to my car I ran into Dave, my former colleague from The Glassmen, who took one look at me and knew I was feeling very bad. I nearly broke down again as he saw right into my pain. Dave had always been a very perceptive person. But I said I had to run, and did, right to my car and another fit of crying as I headed home. Or what was soon to be no longer my home.

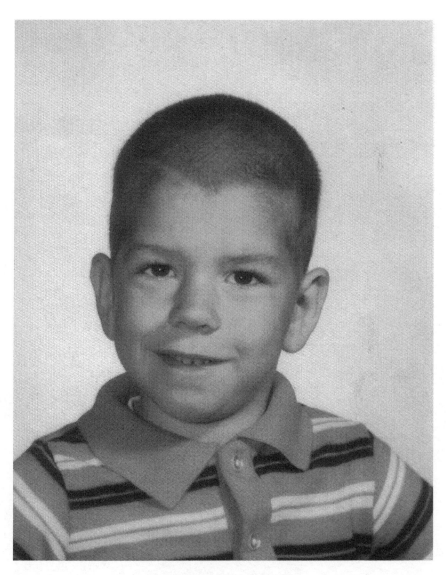

My Kindergarten photo—1964

Mom and I with our new puppy, Zipper, 1965

This is the home near Fort Ord. You can see the tail of my father's '58 Buick behind us.

My father—a very handsome man!

My brother and I at Christmas in 1968, acting weird

In front of our house in Del Ray Oaks. Can you tell I worshiped my father?

Here we are in front of our 2nd Salinas house.

Strong legs! I can never tell when looking at this picture if I've blocked the ball, or been completely fooled by the shooter. I guess I've always wanted to believe the former.

Lessons in professional insurance agent hand-shaking from Dad, the
master of the art! 1982

Mom and Dad at Scott's wedding in 1987. It's just about my favorite
picture of them both. They're so happy.

Increasingly desperate to cure myself, I hid behind this stupid beard for a year and a half in the late 80s. I'm playing a natural horn, the ancestor to the modern valve horn. No valves, so all the note changing takes place with air, lips and hand. Difficult, but great fun!

In the Toledo Symphony, shortly before a concert in 1995.

The photo I sent to the American Horn Competition after winning second prize in 1997.

Bernice took this picture in the summer of 2001. I'd been on hormones for Only 8 months at this point and still had significant electrolysis left before me. When out and around as Stewart, as I had to be 99% of the time, I was beginning to get some funny looks!

Out after a concert in 2002, shortly after going full time. BTW, that's not my cigarette, I just held it for my friend while she took the picture! The first time I saw this photo, I thought, 'whoops, don't wear a white bra with that top again!'

The Toledo Symphony horn section right after Dvorak Symphony No. 9
in early 2002.

PART II

Normal: *Occurring naturally...*

◆

Merriam Webster's Collegiate Dictionary, tenth edition

10

Laying the Foundation

The reality of the impending divorce sent me down into yet another deep depression. Fortunately I got a phone call that, for the most part, lifted me right back out again. The dean of the College of Musical Arts at Bowling Green State University called to offer me the position of instructor of horn. The work was part time, no benefits, but it was a coup for me professionally. The horn teacher had fallen ill and could not teach. He recommended me to the Dean and I started there in January 2000.

I've always enjoyed teaching and looked forward to doing what I could to further the teaching careers of a studio of horn majors. The students were all education majors, meaning they were going to be music teachers. So their desire and commitment to the horn was slight. But some of them had real talent. I'm certain that I enjoyed our work together far more than they enjoyed working with me. The teacher out ill was much loved and I was seen as an intruder, seemingly gleeful in stomping on the territory of a revered and honored icon. At the end of that semester I got some very poor performance reviews from a few of the students, including two threatening to go to other schools if they were forced to study with me again. I believe the student's anger was due to my insistence that they exhibit the most basic of musician's abilities; maintain a key signature, make an acceptable tone, and other boring basics. They wanted to play Strauss and Mozart and I had them working in a Jr. High etude book. They couldn't *play* the pieces in the Jr. High etude book, but they felt that regardless of that fact I should not be insulting them in that way.

The most positive benefit of the job was what it did for my will to live. I rose out of the worst aspects of depression fairly quickly. I also began taking the antidepressant Celexa that month. By the middle of the semester, I felt almost good. The only drawback was the worry about the financial hardships that would come once I'd moved out.

That previous fall my mother had decided to give away a sum of money to her children. I used mine to order a new horn from the Alexander company in Germany. I'd loved their horns since first buying a used one in 1987. I purchased my compensating double from them in 1993. This time, I ordered an even stranger instrument, a full double but built using the French system.

On most horns the valves add length to the horn, thereby providing lower and lower overtone series with which to work. In the French system the first two valves do just that, lower the horn a half or a whole step, but the third valve instead of lowering the horn a step and a half like on the standard design raises the pitch of the entire horn a whole step. This is accomplished because the air is routed through that slide at all times, until the player depresses the valve to cut off that length of pipe. The benefits to a player performing high horn parts are enormous but at the cost of learning a different fingering scheme. Though I struggled somewhat at first, I was using the horn in performances two weeks after I obtained it in February 2000.

Wendy and I arrived at a plateau. We both knew what was coming and we prepared in our own ways for the inevitable split. I continued to meet with Michelle twice monthly. We discussed work, family, my personal history, and the costs and benefits of a possible transsexual transition. She didn't put much stock in the theory that I'd brought this on myself, but that's exactly how I'd felt my whole life. It took a very long time for me to stop believing that I was somehow at fault for being transsexual.

My goal in therapy was to get relief by the best means possible. My house of cards had blown down and I was no longer the outwardly happy, joking, and rather intense guy I'd been up until then. The problem felt crushing. I grieved for a death; *the death of the illusion of my self.*

I was very concerned that I was somehow talking myself into transsexuality, that somehow it represented a path of least resistance and that I was weak in following it. I did not dress. I did not present myself in any way as a woman. And as my depression lifted through medication and therapy all aspects of my life began to work much better, including the way I interacted with my children.

Therapy works best when the patient is willing to think about their topic(s) when away from the couch and off living their life. My way of doing this was to throw open the possibility of gender transition and just contemplate what that might mean. I'd cut my hair the previous October, asking for a real macho kind of 'traditional' cut. It was so short even my colleagues commented. That winter of 2000 I decided there was no harm in letting my hair grow out.

I also began to actively study women. As I looked, not as a lecherous male (I'd never really done that) but as a student, I began to realize that I'd looked at them for years but had repressed the feeling I got when I did so. The feeling was *envy*. I envied women their beauty, grace, and sexiness. Now I could observe them and see through the shame-based reaction that had always closed off my mind. I noticed how they walked, each individual unique but with certain characteristics in common; arms closer to the body, shorter strides, not as 'lumbering' as men walk.

I noticed how they gestured with their arms when speaking or shopping. In a store they wander more. In other words, they don't always charge through the store picking out those things they need, but rather with the knowledge of what they need in their mind, they often browse the store to experience the atmosphere, knowing they'll get what they came for in the end.

Another crucial yet traumatic step is 'coming out', that process of informing all the important people in your life of a significant, if unpopular, fact. I'd told Wendy the previous fall. That was the most important step. But late in the winter of 2000 I was beginning to be distracted by the fact that my family did not know, my mother, brother, and sister. As I've so often done in the past, I sat down one evening in a white heat and composed a letter detailing the depression and its roots in my lifelong gender conflict. I explained in blunt language and short choppy sentences that I could no longer pretend to be the person they'd known, the person I'd created for them and for me. I made no promise of either change or lack of it, but did tell them I would divorce and be soon living back in Toledo alone.

The letters went by regular mail, not trusting people's regularity with checking their email accounts. My mother called two days later. I recall little of the conversation other than she expressed unwavering support for me and sympathy for my struggle. She mentioned that she thought I'd been somewhat sad for many years but had worked hard to cover it over. I cried though I tried hard not to.

My sister and brother both called within a day to say pretty much the same things. I felt so blessed. While a small part of me had hoped that admitting the truth to them would weaken truth's hold on me, I knew immediately that, if anything, I felt freer, determined to see exactly where my gender issues would take me.

So many people who suffer from gender dysphoria also must suffer the loss of family, friends, employment, and income. While I was losing my wife, it was a relationship I felt was weak and flawed from the start. Knowing that I would not lose my birth family helped a little, but I still had the most important people I wanted to keep in my life yet to tell—my children.

Also vitally important was my job. I was attempting to navigate a course that would allow me to remain employed and in good standing with the symphony. I imagined many types of resistance from outright firing (though a local ordinance prohibits firing due to gender expression), to subtle subterfuge (people playing out of tune so I sound bad or coughing loudly just before I'm to make a crucial entrance). As for my office job, I had (and have) no tenure there. I can be fired at any time.

The internet is a powerful tool of information for gender variant persons. I searched almost daily for sites that would offer not just biographies of transsexuals, but pertinent information about how to make a successful transition and the pitfalls that might wait. Some of the best sites include *drbecky.com*; *tsroadmap.com* and *Transsexual Women's Resources*. All are run by transpersons (or former transsexuals; or trans-women, as some like to be called, former indicating that all aspects of transition are complete). Each site listed one facet of transition as more important and more time consuming than all others: electrolysis.

I let my fingers do the walking and called a dozen practitioners. I asked about price and, most importantly, how they felt about removing a man's beard. Some indicated they didn't work on 'those people', but most said it would not be a problem. I heard (erroneously as it turns out!) that of the three methods of electrolysis the best was thermolysis, a method whereby a probe (thin wire) is inserted into the hair follicle and an AC current is sent through the wire electrifying the hair root. This method results in much heat. The other methods are the galvanic method, which employs DC current (using a battery) but creates lye in the hair follicle as a result. It's also quite slow, with each hair taking up to ten seconds to release. Lastly is a method which blends both thermolysis and galvanic.

I chose Haley for two reasons, lowest price and nicest voice. I went for my first session in March of 2000. I scheduled an hour figuring that I'd be in for many, many more if I could stand it (and wanted to), so I might as well not try to enter the pool slowly, one toe at a time, but instead jump right into the deep end. Haley explained the method and how it would work. I knew from tsroadmap.com, Andrea James' exceptionally well-done site, that the average male face has about 30,000 terminal hairs. A terminal hair is one that is dark and comes out wiry as opposed to villous hairs that are white, or nearly clear in some cases, and wispy fine. Andrea's site also quoted the average length of time to clear the face to be 200-300 hours. That meant that some faces took less, but some took more! You do the math: at 1 hour a week, 52 weeks a year, it would take four years to do 200 hours!

I felt I had an above average number of hairs on my face. My beard grew up towards my eyes and I routinely had to shave above the plane of my nose. It also extended very far down on my neck. One of my friends, an ethnic Jewish Egyptian (and very, very hairy) had hair growing down only half as far onto his neck as did I. My father was a jet black-haired person of Irish decent. I must have inherited facial hairiness from him.

The pain of electrolysis is indescribable, but I will attempt to do so anyway. Everyone has had the experience of getting a shot at the doctor's office. The needle is jabbed into the skin and there is a definite point of pain, followed by the injection. With electrolysis, the wire is gently pushed down into the follicle which is already filled with the hair. Since the thickest, coarsest hairs are worked on first, the wire must be thicker than that used on ladies' faces.

The insertion produces some pain, mostly of the pin-prick variety. It's kind of shock in that you don't expect to be pricked by so fine a point. But worse is the operator then sends electricity through the wire to fry the follicle. A sizzling noise accompanies this and many 'T' people refer to receiving electrolysis as 'getting zapped'. "I'm going to get zapped," or "I was at my zapper for 4 hours today and my face is raw."

The electricity produces heat, which inflames the follicle and turns the skin around it red. After the probe is removed the operator will extract the hair using tweezers. If the hair resists leaving the follicle, it is because the electricity did not go to the right places and the hair must be treated again. The operator must re-insert the wire, electrify, tweeze. A good operator only extracts the hair if it gives *no* resistance. There were many, many hairs on my face that required two, three, even up to fifteen zaps before the hair would release. But (there's always a *'but'*), only those hairs in their active growing cycle will be permanently killed and pre-vented from re-growing. Haley estimated that 60% of the hairs she treated in any given session would never come back. That left 40% re-growth due to their not actually growing when she zapped them. Did I mention there is no way to know which ones are growing and which ones are not?

Preparing to go to the zapper was also important. The hair has to be long enough to be grasped by the tweezers so close shaves on zap days are out! One must cultivate the 'Miami Vice' look for months on end.

I spent that first session just getting acquainted with the pain and what for me was worse, the *anticipation* of the pain. But on the second session, I'd had a week to think of the upcoming discomfort.

As I settled myself in Haley's old dental chair, I thought of how best to manage the situation. I could scrap the whole idea, I thought. 'After all, I'm not really a transsexual, I'm just a perverted guy who likes to wear women's clothes.' And co-existing at the same time, this thought: 'I've never wanted anything more in my life...and how silly that I want it.'

We began. Insert, zap, tweeze; insert, zap, tweeze; and on and on. After an hour, I looked at the clock, *and it had only been five minutes.* I knew I was in trouble. Deciding to ignore time I focused on the pain. I lived it; felt it; and explored it. This seemed to work. In anticipation of each probe insertion I would tense up a little. Then when the electricity hit I was kind of ready. But with each hair, I became more and more tense. I started to deep breathe. This only seemed to make it worse. By the 40 minute mark I could hardly draw a breath. Haley became alarmed and said she was going to call 911, thinking I was having a heart attack. Though I'd never had this happen before in any way or situation I was fairly certain I had just panicked, hyperventilated, and caused the problem. However, instead of getting better through understanding, I got worse and worse. My muscles began to lock up. My legs, toes, arms, and fingers were all curled up in complete and total spasm. Finally, even my jaw became so tense I could no longer speak. Holly again insisted on calling 911. I vigorously shook my head 'NO' so she waited. I rolled out of the chair. I could not stand.

From the floor, I grasped a nearby chair and dragged myself into a sitting position. I waved my arms, the hands seemingly sewn on and immobile. I grunted, "Wee shood sdot for doodaaay."

"Damn right," she said.

"Juss waaaid. I'll get bedder," I groaned.

My jaw was the worst. My plan of tensing in anticipation of the zap caused all the muscles in my face, and the rest of my body, to spasm. After waiting in her office for another 15 minutes I was able to pay her and leave, indicating I'd call for another appointment if I wanted one.

She offered some words of advice. "You know, I've known lots of guy...*people*...like you. While I've seen them feel better and better about themselves as they progress through transition, I still say that if you can live with yourself and not do this you're probably better off."

"Sure. You're right," I agreed.

A few hours later all the effects of my episode had subsided completely. A few days later I called Haley to set another appointment. My desire to continue had not abated at all. Over the next two and a half years I would see Haley every week, usually for an hour. But there were periods where I went for two or more hours in one sitting. While my face was quite hairy, the rest of my body seemed to be quite free of the stuff, though my arms had always been dark with hair, and it grew down onto my hands and between the knuckles of my fingers (and toes). But I followed the advice of the internet experts who advised (wisely) that money and time be focused on the facial hair. The amount of facial hair is the most important element in passing as a woman.

By the 4 month mark I was starting to see a lightening of my beard growth. My face was still most definitely a man's. The beard shadow was there at all times, but just a bit less dark than it had been. Haley concentrated on the darkest hairs. As I racked up the hours I began to acclimate to the pain, or the *feelings* as I began to call them.

What we call something is very important. I'd learned this in music. In teaching, if I called a horn playing technical issue a problem it took me far longer to solve it than if I labeled it an *opportunity*.

So with zapping I learned to bear it. Haley would talk almost non-stop and I would listen. The worst parts of the face (for pain) were the upper lip (especially right under the nose), the lip line, and the jaw line. Most everywhere else was quite bearable in comparison. In fact, I seemed to have a whole region of relatively numb areas on my left side. After a few months of noticing this, I realized it probably related to my inability to enjoy chocolate when chewed on that side of my mouth, both situations likely the result of nerve damage caused during the extraction of my wisdom teeth at 19. I'd always felt lucky that a slight problem in enjoying chocolate was my only permanent damage. Some wind musicians have lost the ability to play after wisdom teeth surgery It is unfortunately quite common for nerves to be damaged during that procedure.

By the close of that symphony season in May of 2000 I felt I'd made real progress in the search for myself. Wendy was adamant about the upcoming divorce, but she wanted it to be amicable and thought we could go without lawyers. I agreed.

Michelle, my therapist, disagreed. She felt I was 'ripe for the picking' and by not obtaining counsel was likely to agree to things that I might later regret. She encouraged me to call two acquaintances of hers, faculty advisors for the University of Toledo Legal Clinic. Clinic is a class that law students take to gain experience with real cases. The interns do the work, supervised by one of the two faculty advisors. The clinic was, at that time, very interested in working with sexual minorities; gays, lesbians, bisexual people, and transgendered folks. I met faculty advisor Rob Salem, whom I considered to be my lawyer, in April of 2000 when he agreed they would handle my divorce.

It was decided that I would file. There was no particular strategy, no looming custody battle or huge fight. In fact I felt I should give Wendy just about whatever she wanted. After all, in my mind I was the shameful liar who was abandoning the family. Much as Michelle tried to help me be objective about the issue I was reluctant to see how much I was blaming myself. In my initial meetings with Rob and the first of five interns (for the whole process would take over a year) I asked for his help to do the right thing.

"I know the law is pretty clear about a lot of things," I told him. "But I'm very confused right now about what is the right thing to do. I'm most concerned with doing what's right, and not necessarily what I can legally get away with doing. Do you know what I mean?"

"Absolutely," said Rob. "My concern is that you feel at fault and are willing to agree to be too generous. It's our job to leave you with enough money to live on, and perhaps a bit more. I don't mean that your kids or Wendy will suffer or be put out, but that they'll get a fair settlement. Does that sound alright to you?"

"Of course," I agreed, and showed him some numbers that Wendy had proposed based on figures she got off a website for soon to be divorced wives.

Rob laughed out loud. "How much do you make, St…what would you like us to call you," he asked haltingly.

"Oh, Stewart is fine. I live this way work this way. In fact, I don't even present myself as a woman at all. I may never do that. This is just something I know I've lived with and…well, it's the reason for the split. So please call me Stewart."

"Fine. Wendy's numbers are…how much did you say you made again?"

I told him.

"Well, I can assure you that no court in Ohio would impose those kinds of numbers on anyone. There are quite strict formulas for these kinds of things, and over the next few weeks we'll be collecting information, your estimates, her estimates, tax returns, pay stubs, etc., and we'll come up with some pretty clear numbers, ok?"

I agreed to all his suggestions. They were doing me such a huge favor by taking my case. I think if I'd had to pay a lawyer, I might just have given in to Wendy's considerable requests.

◆   ◆   ◆

My sessions with Michelle often seemed like the meeting of old friends who could tell each other anything. I related the latest news about Wendy's offers, or lack of them, my electrolysis, how work was going, etc. I found the process of therapy most rewarding. Throughout my life I've made nearly all conversations about the other person. I did this to avoid having to talk about myself. Over the years I'd developed into quite a master at getting people to talk about themselves. It's very easy to do, as most people want to talk about themselves more than anything. I was just the opposite. I was the last person I wanted to talk about. But with Michelle I reveled in her attention. She'd heard all my shameful secrets and still seemed eager to talk. I knew that I was paying for that eagerness but I truly believe we had a genuine rapport.

Haley mentioned some former clients a number of times, saying how much she thought I'd enjoy getting to know them. In May of 2000 I finally called one and she agreed to meet me at Blu Jeans, the lesbian bar where the trans community felt most comfortable hanging out. The only day that worked for me was the day before a zap session so I had to go in my *Miami Vice* look; 2-day growth. My head hair was getting to be 'Hollywood' length by then as well. It had been 9 months since I'd had my head nearly shaved.

I met Mavis, Anna, Reena, and Andi; all transsexuals like myself. Only Andi was not full time and curiously, she looked the best. She was the youngest and prettiest of them all. Andi had a corporate job where she worked daily as a man, showing a work ID badge which she willingly passed around the table. I saw her male name along with a picture of a bulky bearded guy who looked as different from Andi as a person could look. It put a fine point on the oblivious nature of most security people that they'd look at that ID, look at Andi, then wave her through as the guy in the photo. Amazing. All of them had decent if not excellent female voices

As we sat at dinner, I recalled my trips to Caesar's Show Bar in 1991 when I first encountered drag queens up close. I'd only recently been reading on the net about the differences between a cross-dressers, transsexuals, and drag queens. They're actually quite different. Cross dressers identify as men, primarily heterosexual men who enjoy (usually for sexual reasons) wearing women's clothes from time to time. They almost uniformly express interest in sex with their wives or girlfriends and simply enjoy a harmless hobby. They're also quite 'readable' when out because they rarely take steps to feminize their bodies in any permanent way. Same with drag queens (except they're gay), though they generally are much, much better at the artifice of female impersonation. A number of beautiful transsexuals (almost all young early transitioners) have come from the ranks of drag queens (which means they never were drag queens, but transsexuals all along). But for the most part, drag queens are gay males who have a male gender identity. They do drag for fun, to attract potential sex partners, and often as a hobby.

In the virtual tour of the world of cross gender expression I'd been taking since the previous summer via the net, I'd seen many photos of transsexuals and knew that they were almost always far better looking than the other two types of gender crossers. This was usually due to electrolysis and hormones. Facial hair, even when shaved closely, causes the skin around the hair follicle to be raised above the plane of the face. People with facial hair, no matter how closely they shave, can never have as smooth a face as a person without facial hair. In our culture, lack of facial hair is seen as a trait that almost always marks one as female.

The other difference, hormones, is not as immediately dramatic, but does create an aura that while difficult to define, is most readily apparent. The face of someone under the influence of testosterone is often more angular, with flatter planes and harder points than a face under the influence of estrogen. Each of the women around the table that evening had soft features, softer than I'd seen at Caesar's eight years before. I could tell they been working at their presentation, but only because I knew so much about the process. One still had some electrolysis yet to accomplish and was letting what hair there was grow out a bit. But even those obvious hairs did not distract (to my eye) from her overwhelming female presentation.

As I listened to the conversations, which mostly centered around transition issues of passing, work relations, and the various hoops they were jumping through; therapy, electrolysis, surgery, voice training etc., I silently compared my current path to theirs. I sought to know whether I felt connected to these people as fellow travelers, as sisters. After only a short time I realized I was in the company of people who'd traveled the same road I had. We'd all lived on the odd side of the gender divide, and it was both comforting and interesting to be with them.

They kindly asked me to outline my story. All were nodding as I related the hazing and teasing of my early childhood, my lonely period, my ability to act the male part once I'd entered high school, and the life long battle with the desire to cross dress. Readers of this book will almost certainly recognize aspects of their own journey as being similar to mine. It's that sense of connection that we seek; the feeling that we're not alone in the world and that we're a part of a shared, if rare and unusual, journey.

"Sandra," (they were kind enough to call me by my preferred name even though I looked nothing like a 'Sandra) "why aren't you dressed?"

"Oh, I'm not dressing these days. I'm too busy. Plus, I go to Haley regularly, sometimes two or three times a week, so I have to let my face grow. That's more important to me now; making progress toward my goals."

They were impressed with that though I was not trying to impress. They were more familiar with transsexuals who dressed and attempted to present as women before they'd achieved much in the way of bodily feminization. I realized from the way they were reacting to my news that my choices were rare, at least in the local community. The better web sites dealing with transition had stern warnings about trying to go full time too soon. I was living that advice. I was taking the necessary steps at a speed I could financially afford and mentally handle. They recognized the maturity of that.

I began to see chinks in the armor my internal shame had built around me, the armor that made it difficult to take credit for the good things in my life. I was taking my steps and thinking them through. It had taken me 40 years to acknowledge the truth. I was not going to collapse now over clothes.

◆   ◆   ◆

Wendy and I limped along living together until one day in early July she approached me with a grim look on her face.

"It's time."

The end of my time at home caught me by surprise. Though I knew it was coming, it somehow did not seem to be real until that very moment.

"I'm under a great deal of stress here," she said. "I think we should get it done. We'll just tell the kids and you should go today."

I paused, thinking. "Ok."

We gathered Betty and Bonnie around the kitchen table. They seemed to know immediately that whatever we were about to say they would not like it. Betty had been sensing something for months and had alluded to divorce a number of times. She seemed to want to rent *The Parent Trap* every weekend, and whenever she'd see two married people arguing she say things like: "You guys don't argue like that, that's why you'll never get a divorce, right?"

Wendy looked at me, letting me know that since this was my fault I had to do it. "As you probably know, I've been quite sad most of the time for the last year or so." They nodded, reluctant to admit to seeing what I'd tried hard to hide. "Sometimes, two married people just cannot remain married forever."

"Are you getting a *divorce*," Betty wailed immediately.

"I'm sorry honey. I'm sorry to both of you, but this is something that must be."

I proceeded to tell them how much I loved them, that I'd see them often, and that we'd still do things together. Wendy and I outlined the initial visitation schedule. We remained cordial to each other. I took the blame for the split without telling them the reason, instead simply saying that I needed to go alone. Wendy had been fairly adamant about that, that the kids be told it was my fault. At the time I would have agreed to almost anything.

Early in our marriage Wendy and I had agreed she should stay home with Betty, then Betty and Bonnie, as long as possible. I continued to find ways to make more and more money and we reaffirmed our pact a number of times over the years. I was not going to back off from that agreement now that I had something I wanted to do for myself. I was committed to Wendy being there for the girls, especially for the following year or so while they adjusted to life without me in the house.

I'd never *really* had my heart broken before. I'd had failed relationships and been told by girlfriends to get lost, but that day I truly understood the meaning of a heart breaking. Those two lovely girls looked as if I'd stomped on their hearts. And the worst part was I could see them working feverously to cover over their feelings and avoid the pain. We'd been best buddies for their entire lives. We played board games, wrestling, and tickling games. We read together as often as possible and I truly enjoyed looking at their work, praising them for their interests and accomplishments. They must have felt betrayed in the worst way. I felt it was my fault. Heartbreak now truly meant something to me.

Wendy and I tried to mitigate their pain somewhat by suggesting a shopping trip. My mother had sent some transition money. She knew that I would be essentially penniless. I told her I was most concerned with the girls and she agreed that buying them beds for my home would be both a great and important thing to do. We all drove over to the furniture store and picked out a set of bunk beds. Then we drove to the Toledo house and toured the yet to be renovated apartment I would occupy. The girls walked through, imagining spending time there. They looked in closets and opened all the doors. Bonnie shouted out that she'd found some great hiding places for hide-and-go-seek.

After our brief tour, we all got back in the car to head back to Swanton. The ride was the quietest one we'd ever taken together. Forty minutes of unbroken silence. When we got home I began to pack. The girls were in their rooms, reading alone, saying nothing. It took me about two hours to throw the essentials in the car. I knew I'd be back for the rest in the coming weeks. In fact, I wanted the excuse to return as often as possible for it would allow me some time to take the kids to the park or just hang with them for some precious moments.

As I was about to drive off Wendy approached me. "What do you expect us to do for money? You've got it all in your account."

"Oh, of course," and without hesitation I wrote her a check for $1500. I also sat down and wrote out checks for all the current pile of bills. This left me with only about $100 for the next week, but I felt it was the right thing to do. Though I'd filed for divorce there was no order for support in place since we'd continued to live together. Rob Salem had warned me that any money I gave her before the courts imposed withholding would be considered a gift to her and not counted as support. I did not care. I was not going to leave my family without financial resources just because the courts were weeks behind. While Rob's warning was prophetic and my decision to give Wendy money then and on one other occasion would in fact cost me later, I cared not at all at the moment of decision what the consequences might be.

I went to the girls. We all began to cry as I grabbed each one in an enormous hug. '*How in God's name,*', I railed in my mind, '*could people do this—voluntarily leave their kids?*" It was tearing me apart, and still does now years later as I write this. They are so innocent, so blameless, yet there I was punishing them.

"I love you Betty," I gasped between sobs

"I love you Bonnie," I choked, hugging them both tightly.

Finally, releasing them, I turned and headed for the car. They both came running after me, screaming—*"Dad, don't go!!!!"*

I grabbed them both up in my arms at once. Their tears, so freely flowing, soaked my neck immediately, as mine soaked theirs. *"I'm so sorry—I'm so sorry,"* I wailed in their ears. I never wanted to leave. But I knew I would. I had to.

This is the most tragic and unforgivable thing I've done. I voluntarily left my children. Even as I write this, I'm crying, sobbing, and wondering what was so dammed important that I had to do that to them.

Transsexuals who carve out a life for themselves in their birth gender role often face these kinds of issues: the pain of extricating themselves from family situations which, while loving and satisfying on a certain level, are ultimately binding and stultifying in their comfort. I truly feel that I was not a whole person as long as I continued to pretend to be Stewart.

I believe Wendy and I would have split whether I ultimately transitioned or not. At that point our marriage was gone. Since I was unable, or should I say unwilling, to fulfill my 'husbandly' duties, Wendy was insistent that she would see me gone from her home. I felt, and still feel, that the divorce was more traumatic and devastating to the children than the later change in my gender role.

11

Living Alone

The house was a wreck. I'd been working on the building for weeks, but only the first floor apartment since I was forcing my friend and tenant to move down there. There was much painting to be done. In that neighborhood one can only find smokers as tenants. The walls and ceiling looked as if someone spewed grease all over everything.

The 2nd floor apartment, where Roger had lived for 9 years, had a variety of problems: crumbling plaster ceilings, a dark and dank kitchen desperately in need of a tear out and re-build, paucity of lighting fixtures, no ceiling fans, and mostly inoperable windows. Roger had not minded the state of the apartment too much. I'd made the rent so low he felt fine there.

My move there provided a great opportunity to get more rent out of Roger by moving him downstairs. Plus, I then had an excuse to get all the needed work done on the 2nd floor apartment. Fortunately my mother was ready to help. She knew that sending me money would only cause half of it to end up in Wendy's pocket since we were still married. She took out a credit card and put my name on as authorized user. I took cash advances for the contractor (ceiling and wall renovations, repairs, etc.) and to buy supplies like paint, ceiling fans, and light fixtures. She also allowed me to buy some appliances; TV, computer, phone, washer, dryer, and vacuum cleaner. I tried to be a smart shopper and looked for deep discounts, including Microsoft's $400 discount offer on appliances when signing up for three years of MSN internet connection.

My brother made a trip out to visit me that summer. I'd not seen Scott since our family reunion in summer 1998. That had been my last gasp as Stewart, the last time I felt on top of the world about my male persona. I insisted he get a motel as I was too embarrassed to have him sleep on the filthy floor in a sleeping bag, as I was doing.

We talked about our past in light of my recent revelations. We ate out every day, saw a movie, and just enjoyed each other's company in a way we'd not done since childhood. Scott and I had never been close.

We'd not been distant so much as just…well, not seemingly in any kind of relationship. We discussed how that had come about. I said it was my doing in every way. I related a story to Scott about a day he'd been upset with me and tried to get through to me that I was somehow detached from him and the whole family.

I said to Scott, "You came downstairs, upset about something. You looked at me and said: 'What's the matter with you! Why can't you just *tell* me what's wrong! I'm your *brother*, for God's sake!' I just looked at you and said something like, 'I don't know what you're talking about'."

"Scott, I was such an asshole, but I tell you, I was as completely closed off from emotion as I could get. I knew you as my brother, as I knew everyone as family, but my feelings only went down to a certain point then stopped completely. That's one reason why dad's death did not seem to bother me too much. Much of why I must follow this path now is that I can no longer stay so emotionally closed. I've got to open up! And as I do I see how omni-present this issue has been in my life."

I felt an ability to see Scott, and be with Scott, in an unencumbered way. Though I was only one year into therapy and had made no decisions on my future (Stewart or Sandra?) I'd healed my soul enough to connect with him like never before. As I hugged him on his departure, I told him I loved him.

What a difficult word: *Love*. Who among us really knows what it means? I'd struggled with that word my entire life. With the weakening of the blinders placed by my false persona, I could see more clearly how I truly felt about people, especially my family. I knew in a new way not only that I loved Scott but what that actually meant. It meant I cared for his welfare, his growth as a human, and that I wanted to be neither a burden nor a narcissistic presence in his life. It is truly love unconditional. It does not matter what he does or doesn't do! I love him. This was the logical extension of the revelation I'd been coming to over the previous year regarding my children.

When I lived in the same home with my kids, it was so easy to take their presence for granted. I *told* them I loved them, and I knew enough to try to not just let that be a word but to make it stand for actions that they would understand: reading to them, taking them to the park, listening when they wanted to talk which often meant stopping what I was currently doing, along with a general willingness to devote time to them. But in my pain I was very self-centered.

Everything they did, said, or seemed to say with body language, got filtered through my warped sense of self. Though I'd been on Celexa for six months at that point, I still felt that based on the Burns depression test I remained mildly depressed. Looking back I can say that was probably due to the stress of moving and the worry about the impact on everyone around me of any future decisions about my life.

At work the summer telemarketing program got off to a rousing start with more callers than in the past calling more people. We called Monday through Thursday 6-9pm. My improved attitude over the previous summer helped to make the attitude in the office more productive, so I had more money in my pocket for electrolysis and therapy. It's interesting how worry is often a self-defeating activity. As my depression lifted, it was much easier to not worry about the future and simply concentrate on the day's tasks. It reminded me of the sage advice of many self-help books I'd read over the years. One particular bit of advice came to mind that summer: *do what you do when you do it*. In other words, be in the moment and only that moment to do the best work. The past is unchangeable while the future is not only in doubt but totally dependent on one's actions in the present. *Now* is the only moment over which one has any control. So seize now, and live those moments to the fullest.

My time away from work was largely spent overseeing the work being done on my home. I hired the contractor that repaired the Swanton house. He was unaware of my 'issues' except that I'd left Wendy and the kids and was living in Toledo. He was happy to get the work. Each ceiling got new drywall covering (about 1000 square feet), he tore out the old kitchen right down to the floor joists, did some electrical work, installed ceiling fans, and gave the walls a new smoother texture. Since contractors never come day after day to work on the same place the house spent the majority of the summer simply waiting for them to return from other jobs. I got them only on rainy days, the few there were.

I repaired windows while they were gone, and when the walls were finished began the long and laborious job of painting. I had no time to get, assemble, and install kitchen cabinets, so for my first 8 months there, I washed dishes in the tub.

I also enjoyed visiting the new acquaintances I'd met through Haley. One day in August 2000 Mavis finally said, "Sandra, why don't you come on down to my house and bring some of your nice clothes. You can dress here and then we'll drive up to *Blu Jeans* and have dinner."

I realized I'd been avoiding the issue of presenting as a woman since entering therapy the previous summer. Part of working my way through the enormous shame and guilt was that I kept looking to books and the internet to tell me what to do. I did not want the responsibility for deciding what I would do. The thought of changing my presentation to the world was so fundamental that I kept dancing around the issue with study.

I got as close to dressing as I could without actually doing it. I took some steps toward transition, including beginning electrolysis, letting my hair grow, leaving my family, and coming out to my birth family. When Mavis called with her invitation, I realized the next step was to don some apparel and see how I felt. And of course see how others treated me.

It was about this time in my therapy that I began to understand what had kept me stuck as Stewart: *I was terribly afraid of what people would think of me.* In fact, many things in my life could be attributed to the inordinate amount of concern I had for the opinions of others.

One day in therapy the wave of realization hit me and I said this to Michelle nearly word for word, "You know, I had everything one can possibly have in this world: I was white, male, in a decent marriage, great kids, good job in a career I love, the respect of a majority of my colleagues, some national recognition for my work…and I wanted to kill myself! How much worse off will I be if I transition?!"

Michelle just smiled and waited for me to answer my own rhetorical question, for which, as she knew, I really did not yet have an answer, but was well on the way to finding. I believe she was simply glad I'd finally discovered the proper question! The steps toward transition I'd been taking were comfortable for me. I enjoyed not only the process of taking them but also the results I was seeing from them. While I was not at all happy about leaving my kids, I had to admit I was much relieved to be separated from Wendy. Just the freedom from sex was enough to make me feel liberated in a way I'd never known.

My entire adult life I'd labored under the belief that a man proves himself by having sex with women. When I was a teen this psychological drive coincided with a physical drive over which I had little control; testosterone was in charge! By my 20s the rampant sex drive had lessened some but my psyche was in need of a manhood booster-shot on a regular basis. Sex recharged that sense of who I thought I was. In my 30s the production of offspring served to prove myself to me, so even though I struggled with greatly increased stress from my gender issues, by and large I was able to continue to maintain my act. By my late 30s nothing seemed to work, not fatherhood, sports, work, projects, competitions, recitals, or sex. I'd run out of options and in my desperation did what I'd been working so hard to avoid; the only thing that could even *conceivably* work: I finally faced up to my problem.

I eagerly drove to Mavis' home with a hastily purchased dress and shoes. She had a nice blond wig. We tried my look with and without the wig.

Mavis said, "well, you look wiggy with it, but your hair's a bit too short without. Six o' one, half a dozen o' the other."

"Let's go with the wig," I said.

I could not believe how good I looked. The 60+ hours of electrolysis (at that time) helped take the worst hairs out of my face and I was able to trowel on enough beard cover to make a nice result (in my opinion…) for the dim light of the bar. We all gathered round another friend's new digital camera for a session of pictures. That was the last time I wore a wig. I'm fortunate to have a fairly full head of hair, so just a few weeks later when we again met at *Blu Jeans*, I left the wig in the box and styled my own hair.

My first night out since 1991 was both a thrill and a disappointment. The thrill was obvious; I was doing it! I'd both dreamed of and dreaded being out as Sandra. I was disappointed because that first taste of some semblance of normality was just that, only a taste. And it was a very artificially sweetened as well. The bar scene is a crude fantasy. In 1991 I soured on it almost immediately. I knew that for me it was not actually the clothes or the scene, it was an identity issue. If I allowed myself to dress then all the other logical dominoes would begin to fall and I'd be facing the issue of transition.

So being out in the bar again in 2000 simply reminded me of why I was in transition. I was in it for me; for my own goals, dreams, and aspirations. I did not get any particular thrill out of 'pretending' to be a woman or 'cross-dressing' (a term I was thoroughly soured on in August of 2000). I was seeking an integration of myself; a resolution of the, first smoldering, then raging inferno of conflict in my soul present since I was very young.

It was about this time that my thinking regarding labels began to evolve into my current position. I brought my ideas to Michelle as I did everything. I told her, "I know people in the 'community' who say loud and proud: 'I'm a woman, hear me roar'. I just don't see that for me. I think that while I'm not and never have been a man really, neither am I a woman. Think of what you yourself have gone through: your childhood with no ambiguity about what you were, puberty and being treated at all times like a girl or woman, the teen years and the obvious and completely different way males and females experience their teens, your adult life….all of it is so completely different from my experience. So I don't think I can ever be 'a woman'. Yet I can see myself living 'as a woman'. Am I making any sense?" That was a common question from me to Michelle, 'am I making any sense'. I was so used to keeping my deepest thoughts inside, that I was never sure I was clear and understandable.

It was immediately after my trip to *Blu Jeans* with my friends that I began to attend my therapy sessions in female attire. I was on no hormones and had had no surgery, yet wherever I went I was seen as a woman, or at least was passable enough to not get hassled.

I remember Michelle's comment the first day I dressed. She opened the door. Her eyes got big; she smiled and said, "*Well*, it's been a *long time coming*, hasn't it?"

12

Double-Life

There was an enormous difference between 1991 and 2000. In '91 my attitude could be classified as 'reluctant acceptance', whereas by 2000 I'd moved far closer to true acceptance. But in 2000 I had far fewer physical attributes to assist in my desire to appear more feminine. I was older with more aged skin. My face also bore the look of someone who'd been through the harrowing effects of depression; droopy, baggy eyes, and a seldom seen smile. But I was *willing* to feel better, I was eager to feel better; I just was not willing to pretend I did before it was true.

That year from fall 2000 through the summer of 2001 I recall as just a 'grinding it out' year. I rarely went out as Sandra, though when I did I really enjoyed myself. I spent most of my time teaching at Bowling Green State University, playing in the orchestra, and working in the office.

Bowling Green hired an additional person to teach the horn for that school year. It was a two part decision on the school's part: having me do all the students would have kicked me into receiving a full time salary and no college will pay adjunct faculty full time money, they'll simply hire another adjunct at relatively low wages. It's much cheaper for the college. The other issue was that a few of the students I'd taught in the winter 2000 semester so hated my style of teaching they threatened to take their educational dollars and 'talent' elsewhere if they were forced to work with me again.

It was my good fortune that they chose one of my favorite local horn players to be the other acting horn professor: Bernice. Bernie had been an extra player with the symphony many times. She was particularly good at what I call the 'crap position': assistant. The assistant sits next to the first horn player and plays only pre-selected portions of the first horn part. The idea is to give the first player enough rest to be able to sound free and relaxed on the solos. Working as my assistant was not a very fun job. I like to play everything. In sports I'd be called a 'ball hog or a 'chucker'. But it's just too rude to hire someone to play then not give them anything to do, so Bernice always got some decent bits to play. She was good because she could match the way I played, even though if were it her part alone she might play it differently. I always appreciated that. The other best player around for assistant was my soon to be ex-wife. The orchestra did continue to hire her, but it became increasingly uncomfortable for me so Bern was getting more and more work from us.

Since Bernice and I had some additional regular contact at Bowling Green we began to talk more. One day after we both finished with lessons she invited me to her home (which was on my way home) for coffee and conversation. We talked about each other's students and the funny things they did (and didn't do!). Then after a short time she said, "So, Stewart, um, do you mind if I ask just why you and Wendy have split?"

I'd been hoping she'd ask. I felt Bernie was a friend and capable of keeping a secret, though it was one she'd not have to keep very long. I told her, "I don't mind at all, as long as you're interested in the real reason, which might be very hard to understand." This piqued her interested; her eyebrows went up!

I'd told a number of people by then; my family, my spouse, my therapist, and perhaps most interestingly, the tenant in my building who's also a friend (he said simply: "Well….everyone's got something." What a guy!). Each telling was kind of a reluctant outpouring of grief-tinged truth. With Bernice I truly wanted to tell.

I began, "Ever since I was small, I've felt strange somehow. For years I could not define what it was, but I've come to know that I wish I'd been born a girl."

She did not look nearly as surprised as I'd expected. She said, "You know, I've seen the hair growth and wondered if maybe you were gay or something. I guess the 'or something' covered it!"

We talked about the issue for another hour or so. She was honest in saying she could not picture me as a woman. I offered that I'd struggled with that part for years. But part of getting un-stuck and becoming whole and sane was to stop caring what I would look like and simply proceed with the right solutions. To this day, Bernice has remained my most steadfast friend and supporter.

My work with Michelle continued and in November of 2000 I asked her for permission to start on hormones: estrogen and the necessary testosterone blocker (a simple common high blood pressure medicine). That recently past summer I'd tried to get a local endocrinologist who sometimes would treat transsexuals to take me on as a patient, but since I went to his office as Stewart (the only way I went anywhere at that time) he was barely civil and expressed his extreme doubts about my seriousness. His reaction was typical of ignorant people. Though he'd done some training at Johns Hopkins, which at the time he was there was noted for their work with transsexuals, he completely associated the condition with dressing in feminine clothing. For him, only men in women's clothes could possibly be serious.

Back in 2000, when I'd first looked into electrolysis, I'd called a local MD who provided that service. I met with her then and she was quite non-plussed by my condition. I did not use her electrolysis services, as Haley was less expensive, but with the idea of getting a prescription for hormones I called her again. Dr. Annette Millie wanted a letter from Michelle before prescribing, which I gave her. I also provided her with a book on the subject: *Feminizing Hormonal Regimens for the Male to Female Transsexual* by Dr. Sheila Kirk.

Estrogen is not nearly the powerful transformative agent as testosterone. Under the influence of testosterone teenaged boys (and female to male transsexuals) find that the vocal cords thicken and lengthen, hair begins to grow more widely, including the face, and the sex drive becomes very strong. Estrogen cannot raise the voice or reverse the growth of facial hair, but it can stop the annoying (to some transsexuals) sex drive and lessen the amount of body hair. Mostly there are some definite, though subtle, effects that estrogen will have on a male body that will in time help to produce the appearance of femininity. The most obvious is breast growth. I felt pain beneath my nipples after 3 weeks, though even today at 3 years on hormones I'm still barely an A cup. The other, even subtler, effects are body fat re-distribution and overall skin softening. These all take a great deal of time; up to 5 years to have full effect.

I came home with my first prescription for 2 daily milligrams of estradiol and 100 milligrams of spironolactone (the blood pressure medication). I eagerly measured each part of my body where I was hoping for change: chest (bust), waist, hips, as well as each large muscle of my body. Estrogen will also, over time, lengthen the thigh muscles, biceps, triceps, etc. which helps with one's overall feminine appearance.

◆   ◆   ◆

That December, I packed my suitcases and headed out to visit my mother in Las Vegas. The orchestra always had a 2-week break around the holidays, and I wanted to visit my mother without the cloud of doubt under which I'd lived for 40 years. I arrived in Las Vegas to find my luggage had not followed me. I was, of course, flying as Stewart. I looked as much like a man as I usually did those days, albeit with longish hair and much less prominent facial hair than a year before. I had to file a missing luggage report. 'No problem," I thought.'

I waited my turn in the long line. Finally a clerk waved me over and I handed her my stubs. "Hi, my luggage was not on the carousel."

"We're sorry about this, Mr. Clark. You know, sometimes the tags get ripped off and we're not sure whose luggage is whose. Just tell us what's in your bags so we'll be sure we've got yours."

Ouch. Though I'd told select people about my issue, I had no interest in telling an airline clerk about it, especially with a dozen people crammed up right behind me wishing I'd hurry the hell up. "Well...," I beat around the bush, "It's a black bag with, you know, clothes in it. Underwear, pants, etc."

"I'm sorry Mr. Clark, we really cannot assist you without knowing more specifics about the contents of your bags."

"Ok," I lowered my voice. "There are three dresses,nice ones too, green, black, and red One's got a little bolero jacket sewn in, you know the kind. There are 6 bras, 6 panties, assorted pantyhose, shoes, curlers, a blow dryer..."

Her eyes got big at the word *dresses* and by *bolero* she was smiling and making accommodating gestures. She was quite cool. They've seen it all in Las Vegas. I got my luggage within a day.

I stayed dressed as Stewart for a day or so, hoping Mom would want to talk about the issue. Though I'd been somewhat angry at her years before during my 20's for the perceived slights she'd inflicted, I'd finally matured, and by my 30s understood that a parent loves their child but is at all times a human being. She never intentionally hurt me.

Forgiveness is a magical thing. While I harbored resentment, *I* was the sick one. In facing my gender issues, I realized I'd used anger at my mother as just another screen behind which I could hide from my identity problems.

My mother was raised in a very conservative Midwestern family. Her father hated FDR for being a 'liberal' and mom had voted Republican her entire life. Both she and my father had routinely told 'queer' jokes and enforced gender norms as much as any couple with a similar upbringing. I think that made dealing with and understanding me more difficult for her. We've spoken of it many times since I came out. She does not understand but she *accepts*, and that is the most loving thing a person can do.

In December of 2000, I was still in my early stages of transition. I had to carefully shave before applying makeup. Now I almost never wear the stuff, and certainly not stick foundation as I had to then. Though when dressed I looked more female than anything else (I hoped!), I was a fashion fright. I'd brought all the things I'd always longed to wear; dresses, skirts, and other generally uncommon clothes for a 41 year old woman visiting the desert at the turn of the century.

I was of two minds about how women dressed. One mind was the guy who'd observed women his whole life. In that mind I knew when women were dressed appropriately and when they were not. But in my other mind, my sense of myself as a woman, I was stuck in an earlier time; the time when I froze my issues in place through denial, shame, and fear. So when I opened the box again after all those years, my sense of how I should look and how I should dress were ready-to-wear from the 70s. Though mom was too kind and compassionate to mention it, I'm sure she was more embarrassed by my clothing choices than perhaps even about the gender issue itself!

My first trip out with my mother while presenting as Sandra coincided with our second luncheon at her favorite casino pub. She had a coupon which offered 2 for 1 lunch. The waiter informed her that in order to use it she had to get it 'validated' at the casino cashier, which was completely on the other side of the building. My mother suffers from Chronic Obstructive Pulmonary Disorder (COPD) and uses oxygen at all times. Her strength and stamina are very limited. She began to get a bit upset by the mix-up. I offered to walk over to get the coupon validated but before I could leave, the waiter offered to do it as well. "That's ok," she told the waiter, "he'll do it," indicating me.

At the pronoun I flinched. I'd never been with people while out as Sandra who'd only known me as Stewart and it was my first encounter with 'pronoun hell' as I've come to call it. Seeing my flinch, Mom got even more flustered. I just hurried away to get the coupon fixed. When I returned she was apologetic, but I stopped her.

"Mom as I told you in my letter back in March, you did not cause this and I expect nothing from you. You have every right to call me Stewart for the rest of your life with the same pronoun you've always used. It's fine. Please don't feel bad." The whole week, I heard only 3 or 4 male pronouns or uses of my old name from her.

◆   ◆   ◆

The orchestra ushered in 2001 with one of my least favorite works to play: Piano Concerto in G by Maurice Ravel. The odd thing is I love the piece, but I hate to play it. Ravel was known for his delicate, soft, and high writing for the horn. We'd played the Ravel on one other occasion and I'd failed to bring off the exposed passage to my satisfaction. This time, I worked harder for more weeks in advance in order to succeed. The first rehearsal was a disaster. I got too nervous. When nervous, the heart races and the breathing becomes too shallow for successful high horn playing. I was able to calm down for the second go at it that night and got through it. The second rehearsal went fine. Even the Friday night performance we passable, but by my standards I felt it was awful. I tend to be an all or nothing artist. It's either just right or crap. So for me, I felt Friday was crap. But since I'd played it worse, much worse, I was not so terribly distraught. But on Saturday night I lost it completely. I tried to finesse the music and in the attempt butchered the solo.

Then, of course, I had to play the rest of the work. The horn is solo for only a moment before the piano takes over again. The horn part fades right back into the texture. When intermission finally arrived I could hardly believe I'd screwed it up so badly. I just sat there while the rest of the orchestra left for a break. Within a minute tears were rolling down my cheeks. I was embarrassed, ashamed, and mad all at the same time.

The other major focus of that year was the process of the divorce. I'd retained the services of the legal clinic, but Wendy had changed lawyers a few times. The nature of divorce is combative. It's been said there are three sides in every divorce; his, hers, and the truth. I make no claim to the truth, only to my position. As Rob continually pointed out, I had to be sure not to give away too much. As Wendy's demands escalated that became easier and easier. The low point was when in response to an offer of mine, which was I admit low, she countered with an offer that asked for both homes and left me no monthly income. 'Ok,' I thought, 'now we're in it.'

We met at court 3 or 4 times to see if we could come to an agreement. We never argued about the child support. In Ohio the amount is fixed by the state based on income. I'd happily agreed to that even before we had lawyers. Our arguments came in regards to how to divide assets and the question of 'spousal support'; alimony as it's often called.

Even though Wendy is more highly educated than I am she'd never really worked in the business world, only part time music jobs and some part time teaching of German at colleges (adjunct only; very, very low wages). I felt some support would be both fair and necessary.

We finally reached our agreement to divorce in early April 2001. Part of that agreement was that we would file a joint tax return for 2000 and split any refund 50/50. There was no wording regarding any possible tax liability.

Wendy called me on the morning of April 15, 2001. "You owe $4000 in taxes. I'm filing an extension but I've figured your tax. If I file separately, I'd owe nothing and if you file separately you'd owe $7000. The tax bill is because you did not have withholding through Bowling Green which was your income, so you have to pay the $4000. I'll be in town later and you can meet me and pick up the extension form."

"But, we agreed to file jointly and I recall we agreed to share the tax…"

"We agreed to split any refund," her voice rose, as it usually did when in an argumentative state. "There will be no refund and the bill is yours. If you're not going to pay it, I'll file my own extension today. What are you going to do?"

"Well, I'm over a barrel here. I'll pay, of course." I took a cash advance on a credit card and filed the extension.

It was also my last semester teaching at Bowling Green. The professor on medical leave had died of ALS, so the school was in a search for a new professor. I applied but was not interviewed. A university teaching position is far different from a performance job. While I felt I'd done well with the students and could continue to improve over time, I was not willing to give up my symphony position. Devoting oneself to the teaching job without the distractions of other employment was an unstated requirement. At BG they wanted all applied faculty to attend the various student performances. With my symphony position that would not be possible for me.

I thought they'd actually take a look at me for the job, but once I'd thought it over more I realized that students are interested in Bowling Green because of the 'family' kind of atmosphere. The applied instrumental faculty become like parents to the students, and what child doesn't want their 'parent' at their performances? For me, it was the necessity of regular performance that kept my skills sharp, giving my teaching the edge I thought it needed to connect with the students. My suggestions to the students were based on real world successes. That didn't sway all the students to listen, of course (college students often feel they know better than their teachers). So with the stress of the gender change, the divorce, the move, and the office job, when I heard I'd been passed over I was actually relieved.

◆   ◆   ◆

My time with the girls was precious. Shortly after I returned from my visit with my mother, I began to feel very badly about not telling them the truth. The court had ordered them into counseling over the divorce and 'my issues', though the therapist was not delving into that as the kids had not yet been told. Both Betty and Bonnie disliked those sessions very much. The therapy seemed to be a kind of forced wound re-opening. We were all working towards a new equilibrium and the therapy was not helping. I'm a huge fan of therapy but the patient has to want it, and the girls did not so it was largely useless.

I'd not told the girls about my situation because Wendy feared the fallout. She worried that they would somehow be irreparably damaged if told. I continued to feel guilty over keeping that secret. I'd told them that I was having my beard removed and they accepted and seemed to understand that.

Betty asked me one day, "Dad, why don't more men have their beards removed. Shaving seems like such a chore."

"Well, you know, most men, I think, like that daily reminder of their manhood. They'd maybe feel funny without it."

"Then why are you having your beard removed?"

So many questions, many of which I was beginning to think they were *not* asking.

Wendy finally relented on the telling, but only for Betty. One weekend night when I had them I asked Betty, my older child, to sit with me after Bonnie had gone to bed.

"You know that I'm getting my beard removed and that I chose to leave you, your sister, and your mother. But I've never really told you why." She looked at me quickly then looked away, saying nothing. Though Betty is a sensitive and caring girl, she'd often expressed dislike of the kind of 'heart to heart' talk I seemed to be beginning.

"There is no easy way to tell you this, so I'll just blurt it out. Ever since I was little, I've felt I should have been a girl. You know I've been seeing my own therapist since the summer of '99 and that's why." I glossed over the fact that for most of my youth, I didn't really *know* that I wished I'd been a girl. That truth, though more complete, would also have been more difficult for her. A 12 year old barely knows who *they* are in the most basic sense. The idea that it can take 40 years to fully understand such a seemingly fundamental part of oneself would be a very hard thing to take indeed.

She asked the appropriate questions: 'What's next,' and 'So you're not going to get married again,' and a few others. I told her over and over to the point of boring her (I'm sure) that I love her so much, and after about an hour she headed off to bed. It was a great relief to have told her. Yet I worried. As I've said, people who objected to my choices usually did so under the guise of the effect it would have on my kids. While I hoped that love and caring would more than make up for the loss of the male role figure in her life I still wondered. How many of us really know what our choices will do to our children?

Some months later, as I was informing people of my situation and the upcoming changes, I received a reply from a lady who said something to this effect: "Well, I'm sure that's all well and good for you, but what about your children. I guess I'm just old fashioned, but where I come from, once you have kids, your life is no longer your own." Her words really stuck with me—*'our lives are no longer our own'*. I thought of those words for days and days before I decided on my opinion.

There is a trend in popular American thought. One sees it in the mother who 'has' to work outside the home, though it means day care for the kids; in the father who 'doesn't have time' to play with the kids; in all the people who make choices that might not be in their children's best interests. The people who exhibit this trend exhibit it, not *because* of these choices, but because they then condemn others for similar choices. They listen to and whole-heartedly agree with a *Dr. Laura*, while at the same time leaving their children with day care. They cheat on their taxes while at the same time espousing a 'get tough' approach from the IRS. How much work is too much if you're a parent? What if more time for your kids comes at the cost of educational opportunities like private school or music lessons? When are personal choices OK and when are they not? I cannot imagine the husband of this lady who criticized me giving up weekend (or weekday) golf outings because 'his life is no longer his own'.

Of course, my choice to remedy my situation was far more life changing than an occasional game of golf and I don't mean to minimize that fact. But to condemn someone with such a broad and sweeping statement as 'you shouldn't do what you're doing because it might harm your kids' to me seems inherently hypocritical.

Many of a parent's choices may in some way harm their children. That is inevitable. Each parent makes decisions based on many factors, including the best interests of children both in the long and the short run. What may be a difficult thing for a child to accept in the short run might be ideal for them in the long run and vice versa. I was making my decisions based on what I felt I needed to do to remain sane and healthy and what my children could live with, handle, and grow with. Were not the children entitled to the most healthy and balanced parent that I could provide? Had I not struggled to deny, repress, and contain my condition for as long as I possibly could?

Like many transsexuals, once I'd given myself permission to change I wanted it to happen immediately. I'd waited 40 years. Why face more waiting? But the interests of my kids necessitated that I remain employed, move relatively slowly, and gradually introduce the changes in a way that would not alarm them too much. Yet at the same time, they deserved to know the truth. I chose a path I felt brought us all the most balance.

With the close of the 2000/2001 symphony season I was again heading into the long lonely summer. When I first began seeing Michelle she noticed how my history was to become less stable and less happy in the summer. This was due primarily to the lack of musical outlets. Also, while actively repressing my gender condition, free time was a chore. Now, with a sense of freedom I'd never known, I actually looked forward to the summer. In June of 2001 I went for my regular visit with Michelle. It would be my last.

She informed me that she had accepted a position as diversity coordinator at Bowling Green State University and would no longer be seeing patients. She reiterated that she would always be available to me for consultations and would be happy to write the necessary letter to any surgeon I might choose in the future. Nearly two years later when I needed that letter, she wrote in it: "We have worked with many transgendered clients over the years and Sandra was by far the most resourceful and educated about her choices and what is involved in GRS (genital reconstruction surgery)…She is one of the most self-motivated and courageous transgendered clients we have had the privilege of working with."

She recommended a few other therapists with whom I could begin in order to get the necessary second opinion. I chose to remain untreated for some time, feeling that I could better direct that money to physical transformation procedures.

Also during that summer, the annual Toledo Symphony telemarketing program began again. By that time in mid 2001, my hair had been growing un-cut for nearly two years. It was quite long and I was beginning to get some strange looks from people when I went about my business as Stewart, including in the hiring and managing of a crew of phone callers. One caller even asked point blank, "So why are you growing your hair?" I equivocated, as I usually did when someone mentioned my hair or swollen face.

Unbeknownst to me, I had been seen while out as Sandra some weeks before. I'd attended a group therapy type of meeting in Ann Arbor Michigan and afterward had stopped at a local bar, *Aut*, to share coffee with some of the other attendees. The owner of the bar was a former Toledo Symphony musician. He was hosting a get together with old friends, one of whom was one of my current orchestra colleagues, who saw me there dressed as Sandra. The rumors started flying then in April 2001. During the summer I finally heard of them from another colleague who, over a beer, asked what was up with me. I told her. She kindly related that while people were talking, it was not vicious, at least not that she'd heard, just concerned.

The rumor mill was also fed when I showed up for the first summer band rehearsal in July. Some transitioning transsexuals will wear their nails long or polished, wear jewelry or even some subtle makeup. I did none of that (aside from shaping my nails). But upon entering the band rehearsal that summer, I later heard that at least one person wondered if they were seeing a transsexual transition right before their eyes.

I felt the gaze of many eyes. I did not know why at first, then remembered: most of those people had not seen me since that last summer concert in August of 2000. By the summer of 2001, I'd been on estrogen for nearly 9 months and had pronounced breast buds (poorly concealed by clothing). Also, my face was much, much clearer of hair than the previous summer, and of course my hair was long.

The process was working!

13

The Tipping Point

It's often said amongst people who've transitioned that despite the best laid plans for when to go full-time (the moment one begins to live in their chosen gender expression mode 24/7), sometimes the date to go full time chooses you. I take that to mean that it becomes too difficult to maintain the birth sex persona and actually more comfortable for all concerned if the person just goes full time in their new role.

Originally, I'd planned to go full time in the summer of 2001 and clearly I was not ready then; too much facial hair, too little change due to hormones, and most importantly simply not mentally prepared. But I was getting very close! In my final sessions with Michelle we discussed the revised time-table, in which I expected to go full time in June of 2002; the end of the following symphony season.

At that time with a year left before the big date, I began to understand that I was *very* close. I felt more comfortable with my body than at any time in my memory. Nine months of estrogen, though at only 2 milligrams per day, had nearly eliminated one of my most hated physical traits, the ubiquitous 'morning stiffness'. That alone was such a huge relief that I was tempted to rush headlong into full time.

But I soon thought better of that and simply worked toward my goals of that summer, which were selling lots of subscriptions via the telemarketing program, seeing the kids as much as possible, and again competing in the American Horn Competition.

I was sensing an odd vibe from my colleagues. The beginning of my unmasking had already happened as previously noted, though I did not know it, and almost certainly was adding to that odd vibe sensing. My discomfort at trying to maintain my birth gender and former persona while at the same time transition to a more real and true expression of m brought about a 'last straw' kind of event.

One day while at the office I seemed to go 'out of my head'. The cause was quite innocuous, as those things often are. It was a piece of mail.

Our office mail is left out for people to pick up off a central counter. Shortly after July 4th, I saw a letter for me, Stewart Clark, on that counter. It was an invitation to a reception following one of our concerts held in a local church. The catch was it was for a concert that had taken place five months before. No biggie, right? It simply got caught under someone's mail pile and was finally uncovered. But I went off the deep end. I think it was the stress of the changes; the deceptions both with my employer and my younger child, and the need to earn as much money as possible.

I quickly fired off a vitriolic email to my friend and boss, "I know I'm not the type of person you all really want at these receptions so from now on, it's not even necessary to invite me, I'll just not be there."

He wrote back, "Stewart, I sense that there is more to your message than can be found in the words. I truly don't understand. Would you like to discuss it?"

I asked to see him immediately.

"So, Stewart, you seem upset. You know, nobody purposefully kept that invitation from you. And what do you mean by 'you're not the kind of person people would want at these kinds of events'!? You're an integral part of our workings here, both in the office and in the orchestra." He paused for a moment, looking deep into my eyes. "Are you all right?"

I just sat there, amazed that all of a sudden here I was, about to tell my employer this most personal and important bit of information.

"Keith, umm, you see…," I began to choke up with tears and emotion. He got that look that many men do when confronted with excess emotion from another man; they sit back and wait, as if to say 'go ahead, I'm not going to add to your troubles and shame by giving you grief over your lack of manliness'.

Through my tears and sobs I found my voice. "Keith, for my whole life, I've wished I were a girl. I'm a transsexual." I hung my head. The importance of this moment had opened up lost pockets of shame and I was awash in their awful oozing. I needed my job very badly, both for the money it provided, and the security of keeping at least one thing in my life the same. Not to mention that I loved playing the horn perhaps more than anything else in my life save my children. I went on with more information, telling him what I planned to do, how long I'd been in therapy, and when things would happen. I promised to bring him some books, and later give him *Trueselves*, as well as Janice Walrod's *Working with a Transsexual*.

Keith, who was and is a very kind and compassionate person, went on with our conversation. "Stewart, I obviously need some time to deal with this, both personally and professionally. But I can say this," and at that point he looked me right in the eye, "I don't see there being any change in your status here. You're a good horn player and a good salesperson. I don't see those things changing. Do you?"

"*No*. I…I can't tell you how much better I feel knowing where I stand with you folks. I'm sure you'll have to tell the boss, but I would like to be able to tell all of my colleagues myself, face to face."

"You're right, I have to tell the boss. But he's the only one I'll tell. Well, my wife."

"Yes, of course. Tell her. This news is too strange to keep to yourself!" I smiled. I'd always liked Keith. He'd been part of the weekly basketball games and I considered him a most likable and accessible person as well as boss.

I left the meeting both elated and afraid. Now it was all going to happen much faster. I knew it. I thought of my full time date eleven months in the future. I was sure my orchestra colleagues would find out within weeks and perhaps even within days. I was also pretty sure no one would be able to avoid talking about this. As I grew used to saying to people after I told them, "If I were you, I'd talk about it too!"

The very next day I began to notice that my office colleagues were looking at me differently. I chalked it up to my imagination. Later that morning I was called in to a meeting with Keith and the big boss.

Our chief executive began, "Well, Stewart…such unusual news. First, let me say we're extremely pleased with your work here in the office. And this…*matter*…will not affect our position towards you in the least. We're 100% behind you. We expect this will improve your life and that you'll be even more effective than you've been."

The meeting went on a bit longer. He got decidedly uncomfortable with talk of details of name change, etc. The boss was gruff, but had a well-deserved reputation for deeply caring about the musicians of the orchestra.

By the next week it was obvious that many of my office colleagues knew. I discovered back in 1991 when I told my sister that such news is the 'unkeepable' secret. Back then, she promptly told half a dozen other people, including my brother's wife. Now history was repeating itself. Within a week of coming out to my immediate supervisor I was scheduling time to meet with each office colleague one on one.

It was a liberating and at the same time frustrating process. To them, I looked pretty much like the Stewart they'd known for ten years, except with longer hair, a more red and swollen face some of the time, and more shapely eyebrows. That summer I re-read a wonderful book by His Holiness The Dali Lama, *The Art of Happiness*. In it he suggests that people work to be more compassionate of others. So I worked to understand how difficult it was, and was going to continue to be, for my colleagues to accept and interact with me. I began using male pronouns on my dog, just to see how hard it is to break the pronoun habit. I imagined myself to be each of my co-workers, some with pronounced religious backgrounds (some of which we're pointedly anti-transsexual).

Perhaps others felt my concern or maybe they're just the world's nicest group of people, but I got numerous emails of encouragement; many remarking on the courage and the difficult journey I must have traveled to get to that point. They too had been engaging in compassionate thinking!

Right after my coming out (it was really more of a 'stumbling out') I was scheduled to play a solo work with the summer band. I played *Villanelle* by Paul Dukas, a popular work for horn. I then settled into my summer routine: office work by day interspersed with practicing, telemarketing in the evening, seeing the kids on Fridays and Saturdays, and more practice for the upcoming competition.

The coming out had a liberating effect on me. I felt freer with breathing, the core element in brass playing. The repertoire for the competition was, for the first round, the first movement of Mozart's Concerto No. 1 and *Adagio and Allegro* by Robert Schumann, a notoriously difficult work due to the fact that in 5 minutes there is very little time when the horn is not playing. The second round was just one piece, a new work composed especially for the event. *Triathalon* is a 3 movement work for horn alone (meaning no piano). Anyone advanced to the finals had their choice of the glorious 2nd Horn Concerto by noted German composer Richard Strauss, or the lesser know (and less interesting) Concerto by British composer Gordon Jacob.

I'd won the second prize in 1997 playing the Strauss in the finals and found that while it's a magnificent work, worthy of twice the time anyone could possibly put in, it was terribly difficult to coordinate with an unfamiliar pianist on a single half hour rehearsal. So I chose the Jacob as it's much easier to coordinate. I also thought I might be the only person (if I got to the finals) playing the Jacob.

Preparation was a joy. I've always enjoyed the challenge of so thoroughly delving into music that its performance is a 'total package'. By that I mean no technical flaws (aside from the occasional 'flub' from which no player is ever free), a well thought out musical plan, and 'inspiration', by which I mean a flair for musical expression.

I hired my friend Jill to assist me in preparing by playing the piano parts for the 3 works with piano. We met half a dozen times before the event, the final time with my colleague and friend Bernice listening. As we finished Bernice simply clapped and shook her head saying, "You can win. That was really, really good!"

"Well, as always, I think winning is out of my hands," I replied. "I just like to concentrate on what I *can* do, which is to play the best way I know how. Winning and losing I leave to the judges. That's their job."

The competition was to be held at the University of Alabama at Tuscaloosa the last weekend in August 2001. My sister, who lives in the Nashville area, invited me to stop over at her home for a long overdue visit. We'd been close since childhood when I would be her confidant, the person in the family to whom she could tell her side of the story in all those conflicts with our parents.

I visited with her and her family on the way down and while it seemed pleasant at the time, the stress and oddness of my gender changes later led to a two year break in our relationship. It was a breaking I enforced for my own comfort. A slight healing has since happened, a fact of which I am quite happy. But for two and a half years after that summer, we had no contact whatsoever.

Once in Tuscaloosa, I finished checking into my hotel and went directly to the university, the site of the competition. I wanted to get a visual picture in my mind of the building; its hallways, rooms, and hopefully the concert hall where we were to compete.

As I walked the halls looking around, I noticed many young people 8-12 years old. It was a Thursday and my guess was they were there to take lessons on various instruments. I was especially happy to see that most of them were black. 'Classical' music is often thought of as a white person's endeavor. Any barrier to black participation is purely cultural. As I approached one group of boys they all stopped their fooling around and stared at me.

As I got close I greeted them. "Hi, how ya'll doin' today?" I'd always found 'ya'll' and 'doin'' to be natural words for me, though I've never really lived in the south.

"Ok," they all seemed to murmur at once, as if they did not quite know what reply to give to that question. I passed them, continuing to walk when I heard a question shouted in my direction.

"Is you a girl?"

I laughed to myself, *'it's working!'* The funniest part was I'd taken my kids to a playground near my home a couple of weeks before. My younger child, Bonnie, did not yet know about my situation, so I was as manly as I could look. While there, the same question was put to me by a young girl, and in exactly the same words. *"Is you a girl?"*

I turned around and returned to them, eager to see if after a second look their suspicions were confirmed—or revised. "Well, what do you think I am," I replied.

"You talk like a man, but you look like a girl. Is you a girl?"

"Yes. I'm a girl." They seemed dissatisfied, but they would have been with either answer. Clearly I did not fit within the patterns they'd observed in all other people they'd ever seen or met. Though I'd injected a clear note of disquiet in their day, I felt very good. It's said if you can pass around children, you're ready. They respond to people's inner vision, or are somehow able to read through any artifice.

That evening all the contestants were to assemble for a group meeting with the judges. It was routine. The judges discussed strategy and mind set, valuable things I'd pretty much already learned. But there was an old friend, James, on the judging panel to whom I'd not discussed my situation and I had an appointment to talk to him after that meeting, so I went.

Also on the panel were a few other people I knew. In fact, I knew them all at least to say hello, having competed on three previous occasions. One was my mentor, Lowell Greer. Two others were Cynthia, who was the runner up for my job in Toledo in 1990, and Robin, with whom I attended the Cincinnati College-Conservatory of Music.

I approached the stage after the meeting ended to find James, my friend and colleague, but before I could reach him, Robin waved me over. "Oh, Stewart. You know, I saw you out there and I thought, 'that's either a *REALLY UGLY WOMAN*.........or it's Stewart'".

I was too amazed and shocked to actually take in what he'd said, so I simply replied, "How ya' doin' Robin. Nice to see you." Since I was about to 'come out' to yet another person, and right before a major international music competition, I put Robin's comment out of my mind and asked James to join me for a moment.

"Jim thanks so much once again for that week in February when I taught all of your students. You've got some wonderful kids there. You're all very lucky indeed."

"Thanks Stewart. They loved their time with you. Many of them still speak of the things they learned in that one hour. *Well,* what can I do for you?"

"*Wellll…,*" I looked away. I was quite loath to tell James as I was pretty sure it would mean the end of all contact between us. Jim was very religious though quite private about it.

"I think it's fairly obvious that something odd is going on with me. I wanted you to hear it from me. I'm a transsexual. In my case that means I wish I'd been born a girl. Because of that, I've left my family and am pursuing a course of gender transition. By this time next year I'll have changed my name to Sandra and will live my entire life looking like, and acting like, someone with that name." I'd learned to speak my piece and shut up.

"God…Stewart…I don't know…," he truly struggled. "This just seems so…sudden. You're…you've been…you've been so normal. What brought this on!?"

It's common for people to think that gender identity confusion is a form of mental illness that begins only some days, weeks, or months before the uninformed friend or family member hears of a loved one's suffering. The idea that GID has been a part of someone, lurking in the shadows and causing a real pain, but a pain invisible to all others, is nearly impossible for the uninformed to believe. I decided to just tell a portion of the story that I thought might sway him to let us remain on good terms.

"Starting around Thanksgiving of '98 I began to slide into a depression, though I didn't really realize it at the time. That's kind of how those things go. But anyway, by the summer of '99 I was seriously suicidal."

"*Oh, God*—I had no idea!"

"Yes. And the reason was this, my transsexuality. I was so terribly ashamed of it." He nodded as if to say, 'why, of course you were ashamed. It is to be ashamed of'. "I started therapy, realizing that the absolute worst thing I can do to my children is to kill myself. I was honest with my therapist. We explored many, many issues and not just transsexuality. Then one day about a year ago, I told her, and I can quote you because it's stayed with me, I find it so relevant to my life now: 'I had everything one can really get in this world; houses, cars, wife, beautiful kids, a career I love, the respect of a majority of my colleagues, some national recognition for my work…and I wanted to kill myself. How much worse off will I be if I transition?'"

"Well, Stewart, what about your children," Jim answered. "Think of what you're going to do to them! I commend you for not committing suicide, but *this*! I…I think you really need to think this over. Perhaps a new therapist would help." James is one of the nicest people I've ever met, yet it was clear his faith called him to condemn me. But he could not do it overtly. Instead he gave saving me his best shot, and then finally closed our conversation with, "All I can say is *God Loves You.*"

Though we engaged in a brief email exchange that fall where he gave me his uncensored opinions on the harm I'm inflicting on my children, James and I no longer have any contact.

Interestingly, just a day or so before I left for Alabama, I'd stopped by Lowell's house. Not only had I studied with Lowell in Cincinnati, but we'd been colleagues in The Toledo Symphony for almost seven years, and neighbors as he lived about a mile from my home. Since he was a judge for the competition as well as a friend, I wanted to tell him before he might hear it from others. After I told him he admitted musicians from the symphony had called him to ask if he knew what was going on with me. People were saying I was going around town in makeup and dressing in drag.

We had an easy talk lasting about fifteen minutes. I said my goodbyes and left. Lowell is such a fair and caring person. Once he knew what my issue was I'm sure he could 'see' the signs of it all over me; the hair, the eyebrows, the lightening of my beard, and other things. I think he assumed it would be obvious to everyone else too. It's a phenomenon I've seen over and over. What we see ourselves we think must be obvious to everyone. So when Lowell arrived at the competition, he pulled aside those who would be judging my performance and told them. His goal was to insure I would be treated fairly by getting out in front of the issue.

Of course, I had no idea he'd done it. So as I came across each judge at some point in the weekend, I was thinking 'he knows nothing other than I look funny'. I trusted in the fact that adults are more capable of denying things so more likely to miss the clues. Plus most of them had not seen me for four years. I felt they were likely to fixate on the very long hair and just attribute any discomfort they might have with me to that.

While believing no one but Lowell and James knew, actually *everyone* knew. Though Lowell only told those judges that would be adjudicating me, it is the 'unkeepable' secret! So those that knew would, of course, tell others. But even so, I had some cordial conversations with the direction of the competition, Steve Gross, and the host, Skip Snead, both of whom were kind, friendly, and complimentary of my work. As for Robin's nasty comment, at the time he said it I just chalked it up to the electrolysis and hormones doing their job and never actually entertained the idea that someone had told him about me, a probability which seems obvious in hindsight.

I did not play on the first full day of competition, having drawn a high number for the first round. My first round would take place on Saturday, the second day of preliminaries. That morning after rising early and putting on my favorite double breasted black blazer (I always felt good in that sport coat!), and warming up at the school, I presented myself to the minder about a half hour before my scheduled time. Competitions are much like auditions in that for the most part it's a lot of sitting around and waiting. Those that have seen the early rounds of *American Idol* may have a good idea of what orchestral auditions or instrumental competitions are all about. I'd tuned carefully with my electronic tuner. That allowed me to simply stride out confidently to the front of the stage, take my bow, nod to the pianist, and begin.

At the appointed moment the pianist and I entered, bowed to the applause, and settled ourselves. I stand when playing solo works. It looks better and presents a more confident and assured air. We began with the Mozart. Music had never come from me so fluidly and effortlessly. The phrasing, carefully thought out over weeks of repetition, felt as if I was composing not simply playing something written long ago. At a point late in the Mozart the pianist took a very minor stumble, and I let that minor flaw distract me. I missed a note. I'm not blaming him. I allowed myself to be distracted by that.

The Schumann was not as good. I did have clarity of tone and sureness of intonation; such simple things when you hear them done well, but very hard won! Literally hundreds of hours of preparation went into those moments. Tens of thousands if you count back to the beginnings of my career. There were more stumbles, totally of my own making. But overall my performance was good enough to make me one of the seven people chosen to play the second round out of a total of about 40 who played in the first round. The second round was scheduled for the afternoon.

Lunch was a solitary affair. I always eat light and alone when I've still got auditioning or competing remaining in my day. The 2nd round was the new work written especially for the competition. When I first began learning the piece some two months before I seriously disliked it thinking it simplistic and 'pseudo-modern'. But a few days before I left for Alabama, I began to see the piece differently. I began to 'get it'. I arrived on stage for round two alone; just me, my horn, and the music (we were allowed to use the printed music after the first round). I made the most of the phrases implied by the notes. Louds were louder; softs were softer; and the audience rewarded me with a call back to the stage when it was over.

After the 2nd round they announced the names of the finalists. They called out a player from Chicago, a player from Los Angeles, and me. I felt very good about that; four trips to the American Horn Competition in 14 years and I'd made finals for every single one of them! Rehearsal with the pianist for the final round was scheduled for that evening. That made for a very long day!

I was tired by the time of the evening run through of the Gordon Jacob concerto. It's a strenuous piece requiring great range, flexibility, and control from the soloist. I was so tired I had to resort to singing through some of the parts while the pianist continued playing. I couldn't play the passages to my satisfaction and felt that the last thing I wanted to be thinking of while trying to sleep was how I 'could not' play certain passages. I *knew* I could perform those passages as long as I was fresh.

Playing a final round, whether for an orchestra job or for a competition, should be fun. If you're there you're obviously qualified. The committee believes you're one of the finest musicians in attendance (at least as demonstrated through the process) and they're eager to be entertained. In my first trip to the American Horn Competition, in 1987, I competed in the University division. I let my mind wander for a moment early in my piece and it unsettled the entire performance. The second time I was there, in 1989 (professional division), I was much better prepared, just not a good enough player to bring off my vision of the work. I'd advanced to the second prize in 1997, so I felt truly ready to win.

Showing bravura confidence through body language had been particularly difficult for me since 1999, but I was so thrilled with having made it back to the finals that I strode out to perform as if I'd never had a care in the world. The Jacob concerto features passages with many notes. It's a more technically demanding work (in my opinion) than the Strauss 2nd Concerto, though the Strauss calls for a musical maturity not even hinted at in the Jacob. Each phrase was coming out beautifully. There were a few errors; mere bumps in the road. Many people think one needs to play 'perfectly' to win. In my trips to the finals I'd never heard flawless playing from any of the winners. I was able to immediately forget errors like an athlete forgets a bad shot. The time for learning from my mistakes was over. Now was the time to make music!

As the end of the work approached I knew I'd done my best. That, to me, is the finest feeling in any endeavor: to know that you've truly done your best. I realistically could not have practiced any more than I did or prepared any more completely.

After finishing, I went out to hear the final candidate play. He was playing the Strauss. Curiously, both the Chicago player and I played the Jacob, so the LA player was the only one to play Strauss. Early in his performance I knew he'd win. He just sounded so good, so *polished*. And the simple fact is that the Strauss is such a better piece than the Jacob. It's very difficult to win unless you play the Strauss. But I'd known that going in and I still wanted to play the Jacob. There were no regrets. For me, it was another second place finish and unlike the first time I finished second, I left feeling very good about that!

14

Heading Down a One-Way Street: Telling Everyone

After returning home I began the tedious task of telling each of my colleagues face to face. I felt that was the best way to let them know that I'm not ashamed of myself any longer. But before I attended to that task I needed to tell my younger daughter Bonnie. Wendy knew I'd informed the symphony back in July. I desperately wanted to be the one to tell Bonnie, but I had to wait until Wendy agreed it was ok. But before I could tell Bonnie Wendy did. I was miffed, but at least Bonnie knew.

The first symphony colleague I told was a violinist who also happened to be the father of one of my students. After a lesson I simply gave him the short version. "I need to inform you of something important. As you may have noticed, my appearance has been changing. That's due to a condition called gender identity disorder. In other words, I'm a transsexual (his eyebrows went way up there). Soon, I'll change my name to Sandra and then eventually I'll conduct my daily life looking like someone with that name. I wanted to tell you first because of my work with your son."

The man looked surprised, saying, "I don't have a problem with it." You're a good teacher. My son likes working with you. I'll need to discuss it with my wife, but I don't see a problem." I smiled. This was easy!

I never saw the boy again. The man called me the next day. "Um...Stewart...I've been talking to my wife and, well...we don't think what you're doing will set a very good example for our son. So..."

I stopped him. "Clay, I understand completely. In fact, I expected it. I hesitated to take your son on as a student when you approached me about this, knowing as I did what was coming and about your fervent religious beliefs (he's a born-again Christian), but I felt that to assume to know what your reaction would be seemed the most awful kind of stereotyping. I decided to leave the decision to you rather than taking it out of your hands without explanation. I've really enjoyed working with your son. Would you like me to recommend a good teacher?"

My only other student also happened to be a member of a very, *very* fundamentalist family. I'd reluctantly taken him on as well some months before. After telling them they not only stopped our lessons but cancelled their subscription to our symphony concerts and began going to the Columbus Symphony instead 2 hours in the opposite direction!

I ended up telling about twenty of my colleagues face to face, mostly the ones I'd worked most closely with; brass and woodwind players. In telling some of the people I knew less well I began to see a pattern. Their eyes would start to look anywhere but at me. In my desire to be compassionate and understanding I felt I could understand why they'd look that way: to them, I was doing something entirely shameful, and who wants to be confronted with evil, shameful things? I gave up and wrote a letter, which I mailed to all of my symphony colleagues. As I wrote the letter, it became obvious to me that I could not continue the limbo-like existence I was in until June of 2002. I had to get the switch done quickly. So I chose to go full time in January 2002.

> As you know, I'm going through what is known as a gender change. I am writing today so you may be aware of some changes that will take place in January 2002. First, I would like to say thank you to the entire Toledo Symphony family as you've all shown me the greatest courtesy and kindness in what have been some difficult times for me in the last few years.
>
> The reasons for this are complex and no definitive etiology (source; cause; reason) exists. The condition has been documented throughout many centuries and in all parts of the world. Different societies have had different responses. The Native Americans simply announced to the entire tribe that 'so-and-so' is now a (woman or man) and will henceforth be recognized as such. Their concept of a person's role in life had much less rigidity than ours.
>
> For some of you, I represent the most grievous of sins and for others I'm simply someone who's doing what is necessary for my life. I would not wish my past on any other person. In my opinion, I was born this way so the usually loaded word 'choice' applies only to my solutions, not to the condition itself.
>
> Some of you may be concerned that your children will 'catch' gender identity disorder. I can remember being in high school when I first heard of Renee Richards, the eye surgeon who also was a great tennis player as she fought for the right to compete in women's professional tennis. None of my friends from high school has gender identity disorder due to hearing of that and I don't

believe seeing her story in the news caused me to be this way. My history with the condition goes back much further than that.

Attitudes are changing around the country regarding contact with people like me. The formerly harsh treatment that transsexual public school teachers received (immediate firing) has now been replaced in some districts by careful education of the school population and their continued presence on campus. My own treatment here has also been of the most exemplary kind.

In a few weeks I will legally change my name to Sandra Clark. In January, I will begin dressing like someone with that name. At that time, I would like to be called by my new name, along with appropriate gender attributions (Miss) and pronouns (she; her; hers). Mistakes in this area are inevitable, so please do not worry—I know you'll be doing the best you can.

I know that some of you are concerned about the possibility of finding yourselves sharing a bathroom with me. Since the beginning of this fall season, I have not used a public men's room near our rehearsals while at work. In January, I will not be using any multiple user women's rooms near our rehearsals. At the Peristyle, I will go either to the Art School second floor, or over to the TSO offices across the street. At the Stranahan, Ray has agreed to open a downstairs room for me to use. At the Franciscan Center, facilities are limited, so I will either travel to another location to use a restroom, or in an emergency, use the ladies room in the lobby. At our run-out and neighborhood concert locations, I will exercise the utmost discretion in finding an appropriate restroom and will never attempt to change clothes in the presence of any other person. I have no need to participate in either group eliminations or group clothes changing.

The first few weeks in January are likely to be interesting to say the least. Feel free to stop by my warm up area, or to come and 'look me over'. I like to think I've got a sense of humor about all this and if I were you, I'd certainly want a good look. Feel free as well to give me any desperately needed fashion advice. I've never been a model of great dressing and that's not likely to change.

My goals at work remain unchanged. I want to be the best possible horn player that I can be. I'm looking forward to continuing an artistic and musical association that has brought me great joy. Should you have any questions, I would love the chance to discuss them with you.

I got some nice supportive notes from a few people; mostly women. The best part was being relieved of the chore of facing so many people who had no idea how to be around me any longer. I thought about what the men in the orchestra must be feeling. How my condition and my choices could call into doubt who they are and the choices they've made. I imagined wives asking their husbands, "How would I know if you feel that way? Look, he hid it from Wendy for years and years. And he seemed so normal." I could imagine the men saying amongst themselves, "Man, what a trip! I thought he was so...*straight.* He never, ever came off as...you know, gay or anything." I imagined parents lying in bed, worrying that their son or daughter might suffer from this, and how would they know?

This all helped me immensely to let them all be who they are, as I wanted them to let me be who I am. I tried to understand that some might be bigoted and closed minded and might no longer want anything to do with me. After ten years in the symphony I knew everyone's name, but had only been on daily 'hello' terms with about half of them anyway. Most of the people who today no longer speak to me didn't really have much to do with me before. Of course at that stressful time, it was very easy to believe that any slight, any perceived lack of courtesy, was a direct result of my situation.

The other big event that fall was, of course, *September 11.* Big world events tend to make people less concerned with their own 'petty' troubles. That happened to me as well. Interestingly, my first reaction was a resurgence of guilt about being transsexual. How like me! After a few hours, I realized how much in the pattern that was; that I would be so neurotic as to take on guilt.

All that day no one got any work done, we simply watched TV or went to our offices and tried to work. We had concerts scheduled for that weekend and were not sure whether we'd go ahead with them or not. And even if we did we wondered about whether the audience would show up. We ended up canceling a week's worth of performances.

After the initial rush of telling everyone I settled back into a routine of work, practice, seeing the kids, electrolysis (I still had lots to go, though I was looking fairly decent most of the time), and home life.

The orchestra began the fall season with a tour de force for orchestra, the *Alpine Symphony* by Richard Strauss. I'd looked the piece over years before and remembered it being nearly impossible to play—*then.* Now, after fifteen years of professional playing, I was more than ready to rise to the occasion. There are numerous exposed passages for first horn, as well as a few long, loud, and high passages for the entire section of 10 horns. I remember that though I did receive some compliments on the performances, there were fewer of them than I used to receive after a difficult and challenging work, before the knowledge of my unusual news.

At my one-year-on-hormones doctor visit in November, Dr. Millie mentioned that she'd invested in a microdermabrasion device. The machine shoots aluminum crystals onto the skin at high speed and vacuums them off again. The idea is to remove the dead skin cells leaving the skin smoother and softer. We began a schedule of weekly sessions, with every other session including a fruit acid peel as well. The goal with these was to peel off the layers of damaged skin. Not only had I suffered skin damage from acne as a teen, but the high heat of thermolysis electrolysis (not the preferred method I now know) had left the areas around my mouth severely pitted with highly visible crevices and holes. Do I make myself sound disgusting and ugly? That's often how I felt. Though I could easily pass (in Toledo it's easier than in more gender knowledgeable places like San Francisco or New York), I also knew I was pretty tough to see for long. My old 'friend' Robin was not far wrong when he called me a really ugly woman.

Early that fall I'd arranged with Rob Salem, my attorney through the UT legal clinic, to file for my change of name. It's a longish process taking up to three months and I wanted that done before I went full time in January 2002. Our court date was scheduled for December 3, 2001. Rob was actually amazed in that most name changes for divorce or child adoption reasons are not scheduled for court dates. They insisted in my case. He felt it was a form of discrimination. I arranged to have Michelle there in case we had to go before the judge to justify this request. One of my transition friends lived in a very rural county an hour from Toledo. During her name change hearing the judge in her case verbally berated her in court for seeking the change, calling her a disgrace to the community. In the end he granted her the change, but felt a right to take a pound of flesh (or soul, in this case) with him as payment for his trouble.

In my case, all my fears were for naught. I never had to go into the court. I was there and waiting to be called, but they ruled without needing to see me. Then I began to run the paper race; getting all documents, bank accounts, records, etc., changed into my new name. Each card, account, etc., required me to out myself to the clerk, either in person, over the phone, or in writing. Some things I'll not change; university diplomas and records for one. I'm not going to be 'stealth' (attempting to live as a regular 'non-transsexual' woman with my past unknown to all who know me). Maintaining my connection to my children is the most important thing in my life. Also, my career depends on having access to my entire work history, all of which I'd earned under the name Stewart.

One interesting event also took place in early December. Betty, my older daughter, was in the Junior Youth Orchestra as a violinist. On the way to drop her at rehearsal I realized I needed to use the bathroom. Restrooms had become something of an issue, as my letter to the orchestra confirmed. While out and about I used the restroom appropriate for the sex in which I was presenting. In other words if I was out as Sandra, I used ladies' rooms and if as Stewart men's rooms. I was never given any trouble in ladies' rooms, but I felt increasingly uncomfortable in men's rooms, places I'd had few occasions to visit in the previous four or five months. On this occasion I was coming from the office so was presenting as Stewart. I steadfastly avoided restrooms near people I knew and I was most careful to not embarrass my children, so never used restrooms at their schools or functions (basketball games, etc.). After dropping her at the rehearsal I headed out to find a fast food restaurant where I could relieve myself.

I stopped at a nearby Arby's. I was dressed as I usually was that fall when at work: jeans (women's, but who can tell?) a neutral top, and because it was December I wore a sweater. I entered and had to walk past the entire ordering counter to get to the restrooms. Since it was 4pm and between meal times no one was there but the employees and me.

As I turned the corner to head to the men's room I heard behind me, "Gaaahd, did you see that? What was *that?!*" There was audible laughter as the bored clerks amused themselves with the real-life version of the awful Saturday Night Live skit *Pat* that walked through their store.

I finished my business, and while washing my hands a big man pushed open the door. Like so many fast food places the restrooms are quite cramped. The door swung open and hit me in the butt. I was at the sink and looked up into the mirror as the door opened. The man looked at my reflection and said, "Oh—sorry," and left. I can only assume he thought he'd stepped into the ladies room or that I'd wrongly used the men's room. In 40 years of being in men's rooms I been hit in the butt many times by doors, but never received that reaction from the guy who did it!

I walked out the door and he was still there waiting to get in. I said nothing, but could see him out of the corner of my eye looking me over as I left. I had to cross the ordering area again to get back to my car. I thought I'd have some fun. "Did you get a good laugh out of me," I asked them while I walked by. They looked like they'd just been caught stealing cookies by their mother. I was treated to more laughter as I left.

◆   ◆   ◆

The December portion of the symphony season is both comforting and aggravating. Like so many other orchestras we always play Christmas music during that time of year. Fortunately, we also schedule some other non-holiday type works to break up the monotony for the musicians. That December Emilie Sargent (the TSO second horn) and I were featured in a double horn concerto on numerous concerts.

Very soon it was the last day of the December symphony season. I rose that morning and put on my usual daily clothes for a December workday—my tuxedo. I arrived at the concert, so like the thousands of other concerts I'd played in my life, full of the excitement of doing what I love while also feeling some fear; the possibility of failure never far from my mind. While in the music time seems to stop. One is simply a part of the art; either great or mediocre. The audience applauds, we stand, they stop…and it's over. I pack up my horn and my accessory bag (tuners, mutes, oil, etc.) and head home. I'll never again attempt to pass myself off as a man.

I reflected on my 42 years on the planet. Understanding of all the events in my life was beginning to come into focus. Many of the things of which I've written were unclear at both the time they happened and in December 2001. Still wary of the 'historical rewriting' aspect of memory, I began to sort through journal writings begun in transition, as well as purely therapeutic writings done during my time with Michelle. I began to write this book.

Obviously I've left out far more than I've included, and in the few pages that follow the same caveat will apply. But I've selected events that seem to reflect a progression from complete ignorance of who I am (don't we all start that way?) to a clearer understanding of myself; of the way I was made and who I have become. It's always that combination, nature and nurture, the age-old debate. What no one may ever know is how much of each. What is the recipe for a transsexual, or anyone else for that matter? We're all largely creatures of self-determined scope and power. We choose everything from whether or not to rise in the morning to every single action we take. That gives power to the 'nurture,' or choice side of the argument. But clearly there are observable patterns in people. That's what gives rise to genetic, brain, hormonal, and chromosomal research; the 'nature' part of the story.

Why are some people mean? Why are some stingy, afraid, shy, gregarious, generous, giving, secretive, whining, winning, losing…why? The truth is we'll never know for certain. It's even speculated that most physical illnesses are primarily psychosomatic; created in reality by mere patterns of thought. Did I create this myself? I still wonder. If I did that creation began very early in my life. I built upon in with every passing moment until it was done—made real—a force and a presence I could no longer deny or repress. So in late December of 2001 I declared my freedom. I was no longer going to deny, hide, and repress this significant part of whom I am. I am, finally, whole.

15

Sandra

Why Sandra? Why not Sally, or Susan, or any other name? Most of us do not choose to exercise choice over our name. Our parents bestow it upon us and we live with it the rest of our lives. In my case I truly loved my given name. Stewart, being an unusual name, had afforded me a sense of uniqueness that I'd come to appreciate over the years, even though the name sometimes brings forth connotations of fey, slightly effeminate persons (mostly due to late night comedy sketches; thanks a lot Michael McDonald and Al Franken!). I knew I'd done the world of Stewarts no favor.

My first priority in a name was that I not choose one belonging to anyone I know or have known. That narrowed down the list considerably. I felt it would be rude to 'take' the name of a valued professional or personal acquaintance. I also feel Sandra is a strong name. I believe I've shown significant strength in dealing with this issue. Not just that I dealt with it at all, but in the *way* that I have. While certain things were unavoidable, like leaving my family, I have not chosen to abandon them or my ex-wife. I've agreed to a fairly heavy level of alimony for a lengthy period of 5 years. I pay 75% of the costs of private schooling along with music and dance lessons. I'm not wealthy. These are choices I make out of love. What I can't do is go out. When not working I'm home. So I felt that I should have a strong but unusual name.

The first day of the rest of my life I hosted a party for some friends from town and from the symphony. We ate chili and played horn quartets. People were kind and brought little gifts; earrings and tea towels; womanly things. Just after Christmas, I took my children to Las Vegas to visit their Grandmother; my mom. I over dressed (how embarrassing to see those pictures now!) and watched my kids squirm over my inappropriate outfits. We enjoyed a short few days. Bonnie had not seen her paternal grandmother since 1998 when she was four years old; hardly old enough to remember her.

Soon we were back in chilly Toledo and it was time to return to work. I'd not been to the office dressed as Sandra to that point and the first Monday in January would be my debut. I chose a dress. I hardly ever wear them anymore, but I'd read on a few websites that during the first few days at work that if one dresses quite femininely co-workers are more likely to get the name and pronouns right. I arrived, booted my computer, and got down to work. Since I'm on a completely different floor from everyone else they did not see me until it was time for some coffee. I walked to the machine, filled my cup, greeted the boss as I went by (he said nothing; not a word), and went back downstairs. I was actually glad that no one dropped by to say 'hey, you look great' or any other lie like that. I thought I looked like me; still large with bad skin. But I felt good.

After a few weeks I overheard one colleague give a 'Sandra fashion report' to a friend over the phone. "Yeah, today he's wearing a black and red dress. *Ha, ha, ha.* Yeah, I know what you mean! Pretty fuckin' amazing if you ask me…No, no, everybody feels like I do about that."

I only heard his part of the conversation, but I was more than willing to fill in the other half with lurid and insulting details. He was only doing what many people were doing; seeing for himself and commenting on the results. I've often wondered what they thought would happen. Did they think I would become so embarrassed I'd give it up and go back? Did they think that the stiffly polite manner many showed me would change my mind?

I decided to not let the discomfort of others bother me. I was the recipient of everyone's comfort for years…and I wanted to kill myself. Now, here I was, transitioned to living as a woman. I recalled my core question of two years before, when I wondered how much worse my life would be if I transitioned. Well, now was the time to find out.

Sometime in that first year, I was overcome with the idea of how monstrous I'd become, or more appropriately, was all along. I think many of us, even if transgendered, grow up with a certain sense of belonging. It comes from the unconditional acceptance we get from others. They grant that acceptance to those who conform. For forty years I accepted all the rules in exchange for that acceptance; for that inclusion in the club of 'ok' people. Now I'd broken that contract. I'd taken on *monstrous* status, or should I say *displayed* that status. And while I was not suffering the overt discrimination that most transsexuals have suffered for decades I was quite aware of the discomfort felt by the people in my life. I penned this little essay for myself as a way of trying to understand the issue.

MONSTER

How strange it is to be reviewing my entire life. I grew up believing that whatever my quirks and faults, I was a good person, a person to be valued by others. Now I know that I am not the person I'd always wanted to be; not the person I thought I should be: I am a monster.

A brilliant thinker on this topic published (on the internet) the text of a speech she gave in San Francisco and I've been thinking of this ever since. Her point was that monster actually means 'abnormal of shape or structure'. A variant definition of monstrous is 'very unnatural or abnormal in shape, type, or character.' The final definition of monster is 'Pathology—a malformed fetus, esp. one with an excess or deficiency of limbs or parts; teratism'.

So we see that the word monster can even be used to describe an innocent baby, albeit an unlucky one. What difference is there between a person like that and me? I can see only physical differences. A 'monstrous' baby's or fetus' monstrosity is obvious to all who ever meet this child. They can adjust their way of dealing with this person from the very beginning and although the poor child may become free of the label of monster through surgery to correct the physical problems, some who've known them the longest may always view them as something of a monster. In the case of a transsexual the monstrosity is of a mental nature as relates to words of the definition like 'abnormal of structure' or 'unnatural...shape, type or character'.

So this is the crux of my problem: how to adjust to not only seeing myself as a monster, but to being seen as a monster? In Shelly's Frankenstein the monster ends up often being more human than the non-monstrous. That theme is not lost on me. I do not believe I am evil only unusual. I cannot point to any treatment I've received and lay any blame for how I'm feeling. In fact I've been treated more than wonderfully. In my case this monstrous nature is completely mine with which to deal.

It's a circle really. I'll be a monster to the extent that I believe I am. Sure, others may think I'm more or less of one, but is that not true of all humanity? I often reflect on the extreme behaviors of men, from pickup driving, beer guzzling, tobacco chewing, peeing Calvin stickered penis size worriers, to corporate liars and one-upmanship criminals on a global scale. Yet I am seen as a monster! Shelly's theme is as relevant today as it was 200 years ago.

Some days are easier than others. Some days I have no trouble accepting myself. Yet there are days like today when I recall the years that I held an entirely different image of my life. Though that image was a dead end, I still retain many of the mental pathways and thinking habits of that person. On days like today they surface, like a dead body in a lake, rising to the top from time to time before some future final decomposition.

It is truly like being a teenager again. Teens must deal with coming to know who they are. I would imagine there are many who, instead do what I did: come to know who they *thought they should be*. That is probably far more prevalent than people actually understanding themselves. The rigorous socialization we all go through makes self-knowledge for the unusual difficult if not impossible. We all grow up with the wish to be like our media stars, our famous pathfinders: J-Lo; Brad Pitt; Sean Connery; Barbara Eden; Puff Daddy; Janet Jackson; etc. Yet all we know of these people is their public face. We don't know how they like their sex. We don't know if they're smart or stupid; ethical or criminal. With the famous we do an even more comprehensive 'filling in the blanks' than we do with each other.

That filling in the blanks phenomenon is no revelation of mine. I thought of it before I read of it, but it's a documented trait. It begins, curiously enough; with our attribution of gender to everyone we meet. Once we 'know' gender, a whole slate of traits gets ascribed to people without any other evidence of their existence. 'Like's to work on cars'; 'nurturing'; 'aggressive'; 'caring': There are dozens, if not hundreds, of traits that we believe others possess on no more information than their physical sex. Yet we all know the fallacy of this as well. Dating is famous for the two parties revealing themselves through conversation, so that each can replace the social blank-filling misinformation with the truth. Love at first sight couples often have the unenviable task of unraveling these misconceptions after marriage instead of before, often leading to the end of the relationship. That is also why coming out as gay is often such a difficult and shocking thing. Homosexuality is usually not one of the traits that people will assign to another upon meeting them. Even gay people do not do that, though they often claim to have what they call 'gay-dar' which amounts to nothing more that a hunch based on physical patterns like speech, dress, and carriage. That's why some gay personal ads will even include the adjective 'straight acting' when they advertise themselves. Who knew, or even guessed, that film heartthrob Rock Hudson was gay?

Take the common phrases 'it takes all kinds to make up the world' or 'whatever floats your boat'. These often repeated lines are meant to indicate a person's willingness to live and let live. Yet am I the only one who feels the dark undercurrent in them? Both leave me with a connotation of perversion, as if the person being commented on expressed some prurience which the speaker wants to move aside in order to get on with business. Today there is more of a live and let live attitude among Americans, especially on the coasts. But the morays and morals of society change slowly.

My first days in the office passed without incident, and a few days later it was time for my first day back in the orchestra. I worked hard to ignore the part of my mind that was screaming, *'they're gonna' hate you!'*

Once again I wore a dress. I thought I'd throw them in the deep end. I walked in early as I usually did and went to my customary place to set my things. Within a few minutes some women had wandered over to say 'welcome Sandra'. That was very nice to hear. One kind lady gave me a gift bag with some makeup and a little diary book. The note said, "just a few things for you. I thought with all that's happening you might like to write down some things to better remember this time. Good Luck!"

As for my children, nothing really changed. I'd dressed almost exclusively as Sandra when with them since the fall of 2001, so they really noticed little difference. One positive was that Wendy finally gave up on making them go to therapy. She realized that not only did they hate it, but it was not achieving any positive benefit. The simple fact was that the kids were dealing with my changes in their own way and in their own time.

I've mentioned that I am continually wary of rewriting history. As much as possible I want to avoid the self-serving pitfalls of memoir writers by shining light on the truth as best I can remember it. As for my children, I'm even more uneasy as regards their well-being. I'm under no illusions that my changes are neutral to them. I know I've affected them *somehow*. The only things I can state with certainty are that *today* they are doing well in school and have friends. They sleep soundly at night. They eat well but not too much. They don't have any excess (or deficit) of emotion. I hope and pray they'll be ok, but the truth is I just don't know.

Back in 1999 and 2000 as I worked through the pros and cons of transition with Michelle I kept coming back to my kids. One truth that is undeniable is that in 1999 and before, the children got a 'sanitized' version of me. They got my created persona, not the me I saw in my soul. By staying unchanged and remaining the male person they'd always known I sent them a message; I taught them a lesson by example. That lesson would be: conform and be what others say you must be, it's the only way. By changing, by embracing a difficult truth, I teach them by example to be true to oneself and to not be defined by the opinions and standards of the group.

I recalled all the cliché ridden Disney animated movies I'd taken them to see—*Aladdin, Beauty and The Beast, Pocahontas, The Little Mermaid, Mulan*, et al; all of them used that very thought as their theme: *be yourself.* Of course, in these films the theme is illustrated by the creation of extreme examples: the bad is really bad and the good is pristine. It was just like Any Rand all over again!

My younger daughter has struggled more with this issue than the older. We were riding in the car one day and out of nowhere Bonnie brought it up. "You know", she said, "the hardest part is when everyone starts talking about their dads."

I heard her loud and clear. She was telling me that this was hard for her; that my choices were making her life more difficult.

I tried to draw her out and let her vent about it a little more. "So, how does that make you feel," I asked in my best imitation of a therapist. But she was done. That was all I was going to get. Most of the time Bonnie let her thoughts simmer out of my sight. But on this occasion they boiled over in my presence. The knives of guilt sliced through my heart all the rest of that day.

I've written how every choice a parent makes has an impact on children, for better or worse. Each time the parent decides between two (or more) options the lives of the children change and go in a different direction than if those choices had not been made or had been different. As I thought of these things there in those first few months of full time, I worried that I was indulging in a 'moral equivalency' argument; that because I had such a stake in feeling good about myself, I was willing to tie myself in knots to justify my actions.

But to attempt to equate all actions parents take would be a grave mistake. I think there are some standards of choice, though as long as humans make them they must by definition by subjective. Poor choices (in my opinion) would include not reading to your children, not providing proper nutrition, physical abuse, verbal abuse, and emotional distance. But where do we stop? Where as parents do we draw a line and say 'these choices are bad but *these* are ok', let alone find some agreement on what constitutes 'abuse'? I now believe that wherever that line is drawn is a self-serving place. One parent may decide it is OK to re-locate over and over to follow the 'ideal' job while another may believe providing a stable and constant home life is too important to do that. Some parents may feel that providing a religious upbringing is too important to let a silly thing like the parent's non-belief get in the way. My parenting is a collection of self-serving choices, I acknowledge that. Some are not seemingly harmful to my children and some choices are unpleasant for them.

I consider my best interests served when my kids get the best education I can provide. Those interests are also served by them having the most stable home life I can imagine; that is one with their mother with regular visits to me and my home. My mother used to say we are here for our children not the other way around. I've tried to keep that in mind.

◆   ◆   ◆

As any transitioned male to female transsexual will tell you, finding a way to speak in a more feminine voice is perhaps the single most difficult task in a process full of difficult tasks. I did not wait until I was full time to begin. I had a slight advantage over others in that I had musical training and could hear the differences in pitch between women's and men's voices. But as I soon discovered, pitch is only a small part of the immediately recognizable differences between voices deemed female and those assigned a male pronoun.

Good examples of low-pitched women's voices are Marlene Dietrich, Della Reese, Grace Jones, and Bea Arthur. No one mistakes these women's voices for male, though the pitch is well below normal female range. These women sound like women, albeit with very low voices. The difference lies in timbre (pronounced 'tamber'). This is often described as the difference between a flute and a trumpet. Both can play the same pitches, but one would never mistake one for the other. They're unique.

So the task for a Male to Female transsexual is to learn how to lighten the timbre of the voice while at the same time speaking in the upper part of one's *natural* vocal range. What never works is the 'Mickey Mouse' falsetto. That type of voice is only used by those who wish to malign us: comedians and actors and water cooler joke tellers. It never works so genuine transsexuals quickly abandon it.

I began training my voice early in my transition in 2000, though I was inconsistent in my efforts and easily frustrated. Once I started venturing out as Sandra in the fall of 2000 I had opportunities to use my 'new' voice, which is really just a variant on my male voice. In person I seemed to do fine, but when using fast food drive ups or the telephone I got 'read out' (called sir).

Once I was full time I had no choice but to employ the best voice I could get and I quickly improved. Certain quirks of feminine speech like rising pitch at the end of a sentence and a slight breathiness I found easier over time. I soon was 'bullet proof' over the phone, but began to notice that I'd slip when I spoke face to face with people I've known for years, especially my children. To this day I feel my voice goes through various stages of 'passing' each day, from bullet proof to really bad. It's a difficult task to master even when one knows what to do.

◆　　　◆　　　◆

During the summer of 2002 I read an ad in The Horn Call, the journal of the International Horn Society (basically a club for horn players), announcing a Western Horn Symposium in Las Vegas October of 2002. Noticing that it was being held in Las Vegas where my mother lived led me to think that if I was invited I could write off a trip to visit her *and* get to play at the workshop. Then I immediately became afraid of what people would think of me, a transsexual, a freak—a *monster*. So right then and there I decided, 'what better reason to try to finagle an invitation than that it scares me to think of receiving it?'

I wrote to the organizer via email and soon received an invitation to attend and be one of the featured artists. He cared not a whit about my personal issues, as long as I was not interested in discussing them with the audience who were only there for music.

I worked up a short 40-minute program based on his guidelines. I opened with *Sur les Cimes* by Bozza, then followed with Sonata No. 2 by Cherubini, *Largo and Allegro* by Frackenpohl, and closed with *Suite for Horn and Piano* by Alec Wilder. I performed the program in Toledo at the symphony office rehearsal hall about a week before going to Las Vegas. Some friends who I'd not seen much in the previous years of turmoil were there, as well as older friends such as Bernice. While the performance went well I knew I'd left room for improvement.

The next week in Las Vegas I fulfilled the promise to myself and not only played a pretty good recital before what is often called the most critical audience, one made up of one's peers, but also a masterclass/lecture on breathing technique.

While in the exhibit room, where national and international merchants displayed their wares, I was approached by two old friends from college and my former teacher, Wendell Rider, whom I'd not seen since the mid 1980s. That was truly a strange experience; I'm sure more so for them than for me! Everyone was very kind, from the host on down to audience members who were complimentary of my concert performance. I never really knew whether everyone knew about me or not and soon I stopped caring. Always wondering what people were thinking was far too tiring to continue for long.

In that first year I slowly learned to trust myself, something I'd never found quite possible in the past. I discovered that happiness really is a choice. We grant it to ourselves. But it's not really possible to find it if we live in a state of constant guilt.

◆   ◆   ◆

The monumental changes I wrought brought pain for others and me. The pain for my kids lied in the fact that I'd ever presented as a man with them in the first place: The *pain* was in the *change*.

Ah, Change! Hundreds of books have been written about change; how humans hate it, avoid it, attempt to inflict it on others, and just generally obsess about it. The 'filling in the blanks' process that we all use to classify people can get part of the blame. Since we don't know most people very well we simply assume a great many things about them, from culinary likes and dislikes (You mean you don't like spaghetti?) to private things we will probably never really know for certain (well of course he likes football, but she must surely hate that he's glued to the TV every Sunday!)

By doing this we impose limits on other people. Of course, it's not us as a singular person who does this; it's us as an aggregate conglomeration of people, i.e.: society, as it's often called. Through the similar actions of many group standards are imposed.

Recently I was listening to ESPN radio. I like sports in general though rarely watch complete games on television. The two morning hosts (a 'radio' person and an ex football player) were discussing a particular football player who, after winning the super bowl, bought his defensive teammates expensive bracelets as gifts. The radio guy was openly laughing at this, inciting everyone to begin wondering about this player's sexual preferences. He indicated that it was inappropriate for a man to give another man a bracelet. The ex football player on the other hand, said he thought it was fine in as much as the gift giver's reason was that a bracelet is made of a chain. The bracelets were given with the express reasoning that the team had been so successful because each link in their 'chain' was so strong. It was a symbolic gesture. The two hosts went back and forth with the radio guy getting more and more vitriolic in his criticism using increased innuendo and derision. My point is that this kind of shaming ritual happens all the time. I would not be surprised if they nearly scripted that 'argument' in order to better entertain their core audience: adult males. Women do this as well; it's not an exclusively male behavior. They criticize other women's makeup, clothing, weight, choice of boyfriends, etc.

◆   ◆   ◆

A surprising benefit of my honesty has been in my work. I read of a sales professional who says the room for improvement is the biggest room around. I like that. Rather than being 'full of myself' like some professional orchestral players, I've mostly gone to the other extreme and found more fault with myself than has been good for me in the short run. I've worked for years on the various technical details of fine horn playing and musicianship. Great performances involve getting to a meditative kind of zone where the music and the methods used to achieve it are joined in a seamless symbiosis that's less about strength and knowledge and more about the soul.

After December of 2001 I began to have nights where everything worked. I'd had them many times before. But after going full time I began to *appreciate* them in a way I'd never previously done. Before, good nights brought out a feeling of 'well, it's about damn time'; a sense of entitlement to greatness that was ugly and quite unbecoming, as if certain amounts of work should guarantee specific results. In reality one can work terribly hard and never achieve high quality work, while another person may hardly work yet nearly effortlessly rise to greatness. To me, that's proof of the existence of talent.

In my case I'd long before realized I do have some talent, but at a level that requires enormous amounts of hard work. So after going full time I began to appreciate my good nights. I was able to stop listening to the inner conversation; the running dialogue in my brain that in the past was almost entirely self-focused. I began to be *grateful*.

I discovered that the old cliché, 'the attitude of gratitude', was the common denominator to my finest work. Whenever I allowed myself to sit on the stage and be thankful for being there; thankful for my colleagues, my employer, and especially for the audience, I found it much more possible to play at my best. Conversely on days when I was too stuck on myself, lamenting any number of personal woes, my work suffered accordingly. I'm still not a flawless player (no one is), but by getting into the attitude of gratitude I'm far freer with every note I play.

Most life histories of transsexuals eventually get around to the topic of surgery, the topic that more than any other aspect of this condition drives a wedge between the sufferer and the general public. In fact the actual genital surgery is quite easily accomplished having been carefully refined over the years. Years before, when I first heard of this surgery, I knew from the reactions of others that I felt far different about the issue than they did. I was not at all revolted by the idea. Even in my deep denial the topic of transsexual genital surgery attracted me and I read every newspaper account and every magazine expose I ever saw with interest and relish albeit completely overlaid with shame.

However my 'dream' of myself, my created persona, was that of a man; a heterosexual man. So in my years of trying to find solace and comfort in that body and life I became increasingly wary of the topic of surgery, as if merely reading about it was a threat to me instead of merely information. When I came out to my sister as a cross-dresser in 1991 the first question out of her mouth was 'do you want a sex change'. My vigorous denial now reminds me of Shakespeare's observation: 'Me think she doth protest too much.'

Once I was being truthful about how I felt and fully engaged in productive therapy I still did not fully embrace surgery. I was receiving electrolysis and getting divorced but I did not rush into any decisions about surgery. I wanted to wait until my life had settled a bit. There was no special moment when I knew that I would have it. The rightness of surgery just seemed to be there after some time. I'd done research on the internet and knew which doctor I wanted to approach first.

I chose Dr. Pierre Brassard in Montreal Canada. He and his business partner (also a plastic surgeon) run a clinic that primarily treats persons with Gender Identity Disorder. I met him in August 2002 for a consultation, and after seeing him face to face and getting a sense of his level of compassion and integrity I scheduled my surgery for June 3, 2003. The international body governing the treatment of transsexuals, the Harry Benjamin International Gender Dysphoria Association, stipulates that candidates for surgery live at least 12 months in their chosen gender role before any genital surgery can be performed.

About midway through my first year full time I began seeing a new therapist, mostly to obtain the necessary second opinion before surgery. Dr. Meiring was (and is) a nice guy. I would imagine many therapists to be professional and courteous but Dr. Meiring was also just plain nice. He was also a long time symphony season ticket holder and amazingly, even though he's a trained gender therapist, he had no idea that the orchestra's first horn player had gone through a gender change over the preceding three years. Once I heard that I worried far less about my life having any negative effect on our audience.

I saw Dr. Meiring about twice a month until the end of the winter of 2003 when I 'graduated', having obtained the surgery date and filed my letters from Michelle and Dr. Meiring. A few evenings before my final session with him I was inspired to write a poem.

I'd never been a writer let alone a poet in my earlier days. Now, post transition, writing has become an outlet and a way for me to understand myself. *Sneetches*, a wonderful story by Dr. Seuss, inspired the gist of this poem. I began at 11pm one night and while it was not finished when I quit at 1am it was nearly complete. I showed it to Dr. Meiring at our last session. I felt like a child showing a good report card from school to an adored parent. I wanted his approval. Mostly I felt good about what the poem said, both in words and theme, but also what it said about its author and where she is at in her life.

As I drove to that final appointment, my mind quickly reviewed the events of the previous 42+ years. From the ignorance of youth, to confusion, to revulsion, to finding an ability to pretend (running to normal), to music, to relationships, to career, to marriage, to parenthood, to my initial awakening in 1991, to a renewed effort at hiding (resuming my run to normal), to being a workaholic, to depression, to finding help, to continuing to struggle with the truth, to coming out (running to normal!), to divorce, to coming out again to the world, to jumping through the transition hoops (electrolysis, hormones, therapy), to going full time, to today; a life filled with truth and fiction, loves and regrets.

We discussed the orchestra, the upcoming surgery in June of 2003, and just generally enjoyed each other's company. Then as the end approached I said, "Dr. Meiring, I wrote a poem just the other day. I'd like you to read it. I don't need praise, but you are welcome to keep that copy if you like. I wrote it for me. It's strange; it hit me like a thunderclap; I just HAD to sit down and write this. I feel it pretty much sums up where I'm at today, which I feel is a pretty good place to be."

Here is the poem. While it is not specifically autobiographical, I think it does fairly represent not only many aspects of my life, but the lives of others like me I've read about in my search for understanding.

What I Say

The baby arrived
all hairless, and soft bones.
They loved it and cradled it
and talked in soft tones.
They nursed it and changed it
and tended its moans.

The baby—it grew,
and soon began talking.
Of Mommy and doo-doo;
of Daddy and dog.
Of cars—of trains—
of planes, boats and fog.

Little by little, it learned many things.
Then one day they told it
that day then they scolded,
for 'wrong' behavior, as they saw it.

"You're our son, don't you see
it's quite obviously clear.
You're a boy, soon a man
and our very own dear.

But it's oh so important
that these behaviors you mend,
and stop saying you're a girl—
on your whole future this depends!"

The child was happy
but soon enough knew,
of all the 'wrong' things
it liked most to do.

'Wrong' things like dolls,
or making stories with toys
and of course playing Barbies,
but of course not with boys.

Then dad sat it down
for a good 'heart-to-heart'.
"Son, you don't understand.
You've got a penis!
You'll grow to be a man.

And this penis, I tell you,
such a marvel to see!
You'll thank me one day.
You can even stand to pee!

This power it gives you is yours,
don't you want it?
Even your mother agrees,
it's God's will, now don't flaunt it."

But the kid now was bigger,
and more confidently healed
of how strongly it felt
that its fate was not sealed.

That penis or not,
it heard life's range of voices.
Reminding it,
of life's range of choices.

"Now son, it seems you just don't understand.
Since you've got a penis,
there's quite a well-laid plan.
Here's all of life's choices—
(ain't it *great* to be a man!)

There's Soldier or Fireman
Shrink, Barber, Cop
Doctor or Lawyer
run a soda pop shop!

But lastly—
and most importantly (but don't fear…)
it's the way that you do things
so people will know you're not queer:

Stand tall and speak loud.
Take charge at all times.
Be confident—and *proud*.
And you'll always be prime.

Be masculine, son—
not quiet, light and fey.
Be heavy—and present
and the world will go your way."

So the child, near grown
heard all with a dark heavy heart.
How could it tell them?
Such unusual news would break them apart!

So out of the love
and respect that they'd won,
it pretended to be a grown man—
the good son.

And the pain was not bad—
at first it was easy.
The love for its family
made it happy and breezy.

But then years and years
of unrelenting exertion,
left it broken and soul-less,
feeling a terrible person.

When, in just about
the worst time of despair
it remembered old feelings
of quiet, calm, and care.

So it looked deep inside
at a view it had had to forgo.
And shined light where none existed
just a short time ago.

And lo and behold,
the truth it remembered!
A man it was not,
though male anatomy gendered.

But was it a woman,
with all that might entail?
"Surely not", she thought quietly,
"that's one test I would fail.

But woman or man
I don't have to be.
I'll just be me,
then see what I see."

And though she looked like a girl
albeit not pretty,
She knew the whole truth now,
and that was just fitting.

For penis or not
in the then or the now,
we are who we say we are
regardless of how.

Indeed. It was my resistance to the idea of being who I am; who I *say* I am; that kept me in place for 40 years. Are not we all taught that who we really are and who we're expected to be are one and the same? Is it at least the truth for many of us? This poem was quite a turning point for me. Before I'd written it I still struggled with being who I am. It was a burden I continued, even living full time as a woman, to wish had not been my fate. But after the poem I found acceptance of myself. Sure, I had some level of acceptance of myself for my entire life. Without that I would probably have been largely incapacitated. But I didn't have a complete and total acceptance of myself; an unconditional love for myself; until after this poem. It may be good or bad poetry, but for me it was effective.

This brings us to wishes. I'd often described my condition as 'wishing I'd been born a girl'. Well, the truth is I was not a girl. I was a boy, then a man, now a...well, let's just say I'm unique! I no longer wish I'd been born a girl. Wiser people than me have said we are whom we are because of where we've been and what we've done. The truth is that without my gender dysphoria I would not be the person I am today. As an unconflicted man would I have had the drive to put in the thousands of hours of practice to become technically proficient on the

French horn? Without the pain of the dysphoria would I have the understanding of loss and sadness that I believe helps me to bring forth those feelings in music? If I'd been born a girl what kind of life would I have had? And most tragically, if I'd been born a girl there would be no Betty or Bonnie!

All these are completely moot questions! *This* is my life! It is what it is, which is what my struggle has really been about: honesty. My life is unusual, not normal by a certain definition but perfectly normal for me. As such I run the risk of being misunderstood far more often than most other people. But now I understand myself, an attribute I lacked for 40 years. And I can say with assurance that being misunderstood by others but truly understanding one's self is far better than the other way around.

Part of being young and ignorant is to fail know that everyone does *not* feel like one does. It takes years before the average person understands enough to know that what they feel in their heart might just be true, even though other people say it's impossible. Some people never learn this and so never even try to do things like climb tall mountains, play the piano, give a speech, run a marathon, or work with children. Anytime we accept a limitation, whether it comes to us from our own minds or the mouths of others, it is we who are limited. While for forty years I accepted the gender limitations my family and society placed on me, fortunately I did not accept limitations in other areas like sports, music, and business. Are we not all a combination of our limitations and our dreams?

Indeed, we really are who we say we are, regardless of how.

Visit Sandra Clark at
Runningtonormal.com
where you can write a review, make a comment, see more photos, and follow links to other websites that discuss gender identity disorder and offer quality advice to those afflicted.

You may email the author at
Sandra@runningtonormal.com

0-595-32558-0

Made in the USA
San Bernardino, CA
03 December 2015